Tom Botts

The Greybeards

T.B. BOTTS

Copyright © 2012 T.B. Botts.

All rights reserved. Written permission must be secured from the publisher to use or reproduce any part of this book, except for brief quotations in critical reviews or articles.

The statements in this book are substantially true; however, names and minor details may have been changed to protect people and situations from accusation or incrimination.

Published in Beaverton, Oregon, by Good Book Publishing.
www.goodbookpublishing.com
V1.1

Printed in the United States of America

TABLE OF CONTENTS

DEDICATION	9
ACKNOWLEDGEMENTS	11
PROLOGUE	13
THE GREYBEARDS	15
WINDY SKAFLESTAD	29
JIM DYBDAHL	44
JAKE WHITE	65
THE HOBBIT	84
ADAM GREENWALD	99
FLOYD PETERSON	135
JERRY AND CAROLINE PETERSON	155
KARL GREENEWALD	172
MIKE MILLS	194
EPILOGUE	208
REFERENCES	212

Dedication

I would like to dedicate this book to the memory of the three Hoonah fishermen who have passed on since I first started writing it. I wish they could have been here to read it.

Robert (Bunny) Lampe

Karl Greenewald

Alf R. (Windy) Skaflestad

Many go fishing all their lives without knowing
that it is not fish they are after.
~Henry David Thoreau

Acknowledgements

I'd like to borrow a line from the movie *Forrest Gump* and admit, "I'm not a smart man." It amazes me that I have a book in front of me; one that I've written. That being said, I'd like to acknowledge the Lord Almighty; this project wouldn't have gotten underway without you. Thank you for your gifts and for opening the doors necessary to accomplish this feat.

My sincere thanks also to each and every one of the fishermen of whom this book is about. I appreciate the time you spent with me during the interview process and especially thank you for sharing your stories and knowledge. Good fishing to you all.

I must also thank my wife, Jan, who faithfully supports my efforts to put to paper tales of my life's experiences and those who have so generously shared theirs. It is said of writing that it is one of the few jobs that can consume so much time and effort with no guarantee of income, and yet she has endured without complaint.

To my friend and editor, Candy Keown, thank you so much, gal. I couldn't have accomplished this without your patient, guiding hand. I treasure your friendship.

Finally, to Daren Lindley and the crew at Good Book Publishing, thanks for taking on this project. I hope it's a winner for all of us.

Prologue

Time — we're all born with an unknown quantity in our account, to be used wisely or squandered, but never to be recaptured. Once a moment has slipped away, it won't return. Time marches on. It's the one thing we can be assured of in this universe. Time doesn't care what the political landscape is or if the environment is changing or about the current state of the economy. Try as we might to slow it down or stop it, time can't be corralled. It slips through our fingers like dry sand and continues on its journey to eternity, one second, one minute, one hour, passing by on an ever-moving train, until another day has come and gone and a new one has begun. What time leaves behind are the experiences of each day that has passed — memories.

This book is a collection of memories of the commercial fishermen who have lived and worked on the sea. Alaska is their residence and Hoonah their homeport. They display the name proudly on the sterns of their vessels for all the world to see. My desire was to have a record, a document of some sort, before these folks pass on and their memories are lost forever. When the fishermen mentioned here are laid to rest, there will be a written testimony of the struggles they endured and the joy they felt as they harvested the sea.

From the time that the first Tlingit stepped ashore until the present day, the residents of Hoonah have drawn

The Greybeards

life from the sea. Fishing, whether for subsistence, livelihood or sport, has always played an important part here. I won't attempt to fill these pages with facts about climate or population or the local wildlife. You can find those facts with a simple search on the Internet. Some of that information may come up in the course of the interviews that I've done, but what I have endeavored to do is expose the reader to the things that you won't see in ads designed to draw in crowds of tourists.

For the most part, I've attempted to let these fishermen relay their stories in their own words. Their voices should be heard above my own, without undue editing or political correctness. Alaskans are known for speaking their minds, and if someone should be offended by their comments, then perhaps this book would be best left unopened. If, however, you want an unabashed look at one small Alaskan coastal community and a chance to hear the stories of those for whom fishing has been a lifestyle, please continue on. My hope is that when you're finished reading this you'll have a better understanding of the men and women who have lived here and remember how life used to be.

Hoonah is a fishing village, and there are a number of fascinating fishermen here, all of whom have stories of adventure and danger and triumph. If I were to interview every resident who made a living off of the sea, I would never finish. To the many fine folks who I was unable to get to, please accept my apologies. I simply ran out of time.

The Greybeards

The tattle tale jumps and jerks violently, and I look out the pilot house window in time to see the springs that connect to the trolling wire on the port side stretched as far as they could go. A big king salmon had hit my line, and my heart was pounding like the spring that signals that I have a fish on. My initial reaction was to run to the cockpit and engage the gurdy that will reel the fish to the surface, but I'd jumped the gun enough times to know that rushing out to gaff it might result in a fish that's still fresh and rowdy and hard to bring aboard. I've lost more than a few fish because I got too anxious to see what bit my hook. Occasionally the fish has come to the surface almost docile, like it intends to cooperate, and with a silly grin on my face and my heart hammering, I start to pull in the line, hand over hand, slowly trying to coax it to my vessel, eyeballing its beauty and doing a mental calculation of its value. Then, without warning, it turns from the boat and in an impressive show of power runs the length of the line it's attached to, sometimes snapping the monofilament like cheap thread, other times ripping the hook from its mouth. Either way it's gone like the smile I'd just sported, and I start wondering why I didn't just wait and give it a little time to soak — a few minutes to drag the 50-pound lead cannonball around and tire itself out. Sure, there have been times when I waited, only to pull up an empty hook,

The Greybeards

but more often than not, patience has paid off. Such was the case this time. I turn on the hydraulics and walk slowly and deliberately back to the stern of the boat and hop down into the cockpit, looking up at the troll springs as they stretch with each new run the king takes. He's starting to tire. A few more minutes and I'll bring him up.

If I still smoked, I might have lit up and enjoyed a cigarette before hauling the gear in. Years ago, I'd observed Joar Savland, one of the local highliners, pulling cohos at North Inian Pass. Born in Norway, he had migrated to Hoonah as a young man. He worked for a time as a logger before launching his career as a commercial fisherman. He learned the ropes and distinguished himself as a professional. I was trolling behind him and watched as he slowly made his way to the stern, casually looked at the tips of his poles and reached in his pocket for a Pall Mall. In the years that I'd known him I'd never seen him rush to do anything. He worked slowly and methodically and with a patience that years of experience had imparted to him. With a pair of binoculars plastered to my eyes, I could see his springs pounding, and I was amazed at the tranquility that he seemed to possess. I, on the other hand, was practically peeing my pants with anxiety — and it wasn't even my boat! How could he possibly be so calm when there were fish on the line? He finally tossed his smoke and engaged the gurdies, pulling in one fish after another. If he had rushed to pull the gear aboard, as was my habit, he probably would have missed the clatter of fish. Cohos in particular are attracted to the

The Greybeards

line when they see their buddies thrashing around. Patience when fishing can prove to be most profitable. It was a good lesson, but one that I didn't learn for a number of years. For some reason, I stubbornly clung to the idea that I knew what I was doing, though the fish tickets proved otherwise.

Over the course of 30 years, I've talked to a number of the local fishermen, hoping to glean some tidbit of knowledge that I could put to use. Back in the early days, when I was just starting out, I fished out of a 14-foot skiff with little more than an intense desire to catch the silvery bright salmon that ply the local waters. In those days, I dogged my fellow skiff fishermen, following them to the dock, watching them unload their catch, eyeballing their gear and engaging them in friendly conversation, trying to discover the secret of why they caught so many more fish than me.

We were mainly rod fishermen then, running two or maybe three rods, one off each side of the boat and sometimes one off the stern, out in all kinds of weather, often without even the shelter of a canvas top.

One of the toughest fishermen I've ever met was George Hall; he was determined, patient and seemingly unaffected by the harsh elements. Perhaps it was attributable to his Tlingit heritage. His ancestors came from Glacier Bay, where extreme weather was a normal part of life. You had to adapt or die. I was always amazed to see him trolling by the dock in an open skiff, rods over the side, with snow pelting his body and one gloveless

The Greybeards

hand holding the tiller. He could fish like that for hours — a knit cap for his close-cropped grey head, a set of insulated brown coveralls and a pair of rubber boots his only protection against the weather. I don't even remember him having a seat to lean back against. More often than not he brought in fish, too. I would have liked to have known him better. He's long since passed away. At one time the new harbor had a plaque down near the harbormaster's shack declaring it to be the George Hall Memorial Harbor. In a town filled with many a good fisherman, I think it is telling that the harbor was named after him.

Charlie Jack Sr. was another skiff fisherman, though in his early years he skippered the seine boat *Tennessee*. He frequently came in to the store where I worked and would strike up a conversation about fishing. Charlie repeatedly told of his trips on the *Tennessee* and the time he was the high boat in a particularly poor season. As the stories unfolded, his eyes would light up, and a smile would creep across his brown, lined face. He was proud to be a fisherman and proud to be from Hoonah.

Though he was deaf for the most part, he could more or less read lips, and if all else failed, he usually had a pad of paper that you could write on. Perhaps because of his deafness he didn't enunciate his words well, and when he spoke it sounded like he wasn't moving his lips, but he finished almost every sentence with a sincere laugh, and it was impossible not to like the guy.

I often watched him shuffling down the dock toward

The Greybeards

the downtown float where he kept his small boat tethered. He walked slowly and stiffly, grasping the rails of the gangplank and working his way downward. His movements were deliberate and unhurried as he made room in the cramped confines of his skiff. Once all was situated where he wanted it, the gas cans near the middle, the rods along the sides of the boat, the bait on the seat in front of him, he would pull the cord on the small outboard and leave the dock, motoring slowly toward the fishing grounds, a trail of blue-white exhaust swirling in his wake.

The last few years that he fished, he had switched from rods to downriggers, thin spooled reel-like devices with wire line used for trolling. They had a 3-foot boom attached that kept the wire away from the boat while fishing. His were modified to work like hand gurdies, the commercial prototype that the downriggers were modeled after. He could fish more lines at the same time and go deeper than with rods, and frequently multiple fish could be caught simultaneously.

On days when I was fishing near him, I would watch with amusement when a fish stuck. He would rise like lightning from his seat and start to crank up the line. I was almost as excited as he was. He was transformed from an old man to a youth again, and the joy he got from catching a salmon was contagious. I shared both in the thrill of the catch and the agony of losing the quarry, knowing full well that it could be hours before another fish would strike.

Occasionally I would watch him pulling up to the cold storage float at the end of the day, and I would drop by to

The Greybeards

see how he had done and to give him a hand tying up his boat. I'd motion for him to toss me his rope, which he did, while throwing the engine into reverse to pull the stern closer.

"Tom! You're a good man, Tom!" he would say through what sounded like clenched teeth.

"How did you do today, Charlie?" I'd ask.

Unable to hear me, he often would start a conversation totally unrelated to the question I had just asked.

"You're going out to the farm today?"

I would nod or shake my head and try again, pointing toward the fish box and raising my hands, palm up.

"You're going fishing, Tom?"

Again I would nod and point back at the box.

"Ahhh, not many today, Tom, small tides." Then, true to his nature, he would reach down under his seat and pull out a package of whatever hoochie he was using to show me. Unlike some fishermen, Charlie was generous with his information.

"You try these. They're the best!" he would exclaim and then laugh and shake his head, affirming his belief. I would make a mental note to check the shelves of the store and see if perchance there were any hoochies left that Charlie considered the latest hot bait.

In the time that I knew him he showed me different ways to rig the bait, like how to run a small swivel placed just the right distance from the end of the flasher. Once the swivel was passed through the rod, a makeshift snap with a 1-pound lead cannonball was hung on the line and

The Greybeards

lowered to whatever depth I wanted to fish. When a fish hit, I reeled up the cannonball, opened the snap and started fighting the fish unencumbered. The swivel passed right through the eyes of the rod and onto the reel. I never would have thought of such a thing in a hundred years, but Charlie was from a long line of people who have lived off the sea, who had to learn how to fish in order to survive.

Charlie, like George, has been gone quite a while. In fact, until the other day when I was writing this chapter, I hadn't thought of him for a long time, which is part of the reason I'm writing this book. I don't want to forget Charlie or George or any of the other men who have made Hoonah their home and fishing their way of life to some degree or another.

Though I've tried to pin down several of the local anglers for an interview, they've proven to be as elusive as a king salmon in winter. Several of the old-timers have held to the practice of secrecy. Red Spayth was one such fellow. He used to own the *Miss Debra* and was known for his prowess fishing for spring kings out by Graves Harbor on the outside coast. I asked several times if I could interview him and even offered a steak dinner, but he thought I only wanted to know his secrets. While that may be partially true, I was mainly interested in any stories he might have told. Anyone who has spent any time fishing in Alaska has tales of huge scores or horrible weather or animals he or she has encountered. Just spending time on the water here makes it likely that you'll end up with

The Greybeards

something fascinating to recount. I remember Red describing a rendezvous with a Humpback whale that came under his boat and lifted it up while he was fishing at Homeshore for cohos one year. I know he's got dozens more stories that would entertain and delight, but I'm afraid he'll go to the grave without sharing them. Though he's sold his boat and no longer fishes, his wealth of knowledge will die with him — what a shame.

Another such fisherman is Skippy Rude. He's a few months shy of his 90th birthday as of this writing. He fished his boat, the *Shelise and Cole*, again this year with the help of his grandson. His body is wearing out, but his mind is sharp as a tack. He started fishing with his dad when he was a boy on his father's boat, the *Beulah*. I remember him saying that every morning his father sent him down to the galley to fix him bacon and eggs while the boat pitched and rolled out on the ocean, with a thick blanket of fog adding to the misery. He claimed he always got seasick while he was cooking, but his father didn't care. He wanted his breakfast. It would seem that after such a bad experience growing up that Skip would have chosen a different profession, but for 75 years he's made his living from the sea. While he will talk freely at the dock of days gone by, he is reluctant to be recorded. I wish I could change his mind, but I think it would be futile to try.

There are a few skiff fishermen here who still manage to carve out a living in their small boats. I haven't had much success pinning them down, either, and though for the past several years they've agreed to do an interview, I

The Greybeards

have my doubts as to whether it will ever happen. Unforeseen and unfortunate health issues have plagued two of the more successful rod anglers. Mike Mills had some type of heart pump implanted a short time ago after a bout of incidents where he passed out. His cousin, Robert Lampe, was recently diagnosed with cancer. Here in Hoonah, he's affectionately known as Bunny. Don't ask me how he came by that name; it's one of the many questions I'd love to ask him.

When I first started trolling, I spent many a day fishing alongside Bunny. When we passed each other in our skiffs, he would invariably yell, "How many, Tom?" Then he would hold up his fingers to show me his numbers, sometimes holding his hands apart to indicate the size. He never seemed to catch any small ones, or at least he never spoke about them. His fish were always "slabs." I never met anyone who enjoyed fishing as much as Bunny did. Whenever he had a fish on, he let out a whoop and started cranking it in.

Years ago, we were fishing alongside each other at Point Sophia for cohos. When he passed me, he yelled, "I told myself I can't have another beer until I catch number 34!" Not too much time had passed before I heard a loud "Waahooo!" I turned in time to see him pop the top on another cold one. He brought such passion and joy to his profession that it was fun just to watch him.

Fishermen are like the quarry they catch. Usually they gather in the same places, often at the top of the dock. It starts out with one fellow leaning against the railing or

The Greybeards

stopping at the edge of the ramp, then another shows up on the way to his boat. They start talking and soon there's another and another, and before you know it, you have a whole school of them. If you're lucky there will be at least one in the group who's been around long enough to remember ol' so and so. They were part of the brotherhood of fishermen — guys who aren't around anymore, but you wish they were. They were characters who earned the right to be resurrected and discussed again, perhaps because of their skills, often because of some off-the-wall habits or their boats or whatever it was that made them stand out. You hope that someday when a group of your fellow anglers school up, they'll laugh and slap their knees and start talking about the time you did this or that, and you'll be ol' Floyd or ol' Kenny or ol' Gus.

It seems that whenever fishermen gather together the stories come out; like men searching their tackle boxes for a favorite lure, the tales emerge. They are dusted off, sharpened and told again, sometimes embellished, sometimes missing a detail or two, but always entertaining, and if you have the time, it's worth the while to stop and take a seat on the bull rail and listen.

I was down at the harbor just the other day. It was early March, and we were caught in nature's struggle between the last snows of winter and the first signs of spring.

Winters in Alaska can seem to last forever, and if you're not fond of the cold or snow, like me, they appear to last even longer.

The Greybeards

I happened to be walking past the parking lot when I saw Kenny Schoonover's truck. Kenny was leaning out the window, puffing on a cigarette and talking to Floyd Peterson and Kim Thompson. Three fishermen gathered — the school was starting to form.

I didn't need to be anywhere soon, and I wanted to say hi, so I sauntered on over. It's not like I had a choice, really. There is something in the genes of fishermen that compels them to gather with their fellow anglers. Usually it's fun, but sometimes it's downright annoying, especially when you're working on the boat, trying to get ready for the season. Almost without fail, the sound of a sander or caulking hammer or drill will draw a group of observers from all the neighboring floats where they will gather like crows on a dumpster. Some guys have an unnatural ability to keep working, but that's kind of rare. Seldom do the observers actually lend a hand toward the project, though there is usually no shortage of advice about how to do what you are doing better than the way you are doing it. Sometimes if the gathering occurs in the morning, you can still salvage the day. If it happens in the afternoon and there is beer present in the hands of the observer, it's almost a guarantee that the day will be shot. The presence of beer on the float is like a calling card for the BSers to congregate. You have to put in an 18-hour day just to get a few hours of work done. It always kind of amazes me that anyone gets out to fish.

On this particular day, I don't think anyone was really working on his boat. It was still a little chilly out, but there

The Greybeards

was a promise of spring in the air. The longer days induce you to at least make an appearance at the harbor and look at the boat, see who's around and who might be out making a halibut set or dragging for a winter king.

Kim and I shook hands, and someone mentioned a previous book I'd written. I said I wanted to do a book on the local fishermen, and that started a conversation between Kenny and Floyd. Both men are known for their fishing prowess, and between the two, volumes could be written on the art of catching fish. Today, though, there was no talk of fishing methods. Instead, the conversation turned to characters from the past — men who are long since gone, but certainly not forgotten.

"Remember ol' Charlie on the *Rough Rider*?" asked Kenny as he took a drag on his cigarette. Of course, the only one old enough to remember him was Floyd, but that was okay. I was just along for the ride.

"Hell, yes, I remember him!" Floyd replied. "I was just a boy when he was around. I remember one time he come into town and tied up at the old Thompson float. He'd made $300 fishing and wanted to go into Juneau and spend it. He called me over and told me to watch the boat for him. 'Take it out if you want to,' he said. 'You can't hurt anything.' Well, I wanted to go watch a movie that afternoon. They used to show movies in the old Quonset hut down by the ANB Hall, so I checked it before I went and watched the show. A couple hours later, I came out and went down to check on the boat, and only the tops of the trolling poles were showing — the boat sank right

The Greybeards

there at the dock! The old *Rough Rider* leaked like a sieve and was kept afloat by an automatic bilge pump. As soon as the battery went dead, down she went. Boy, I was kind of scared. God, I'm watching Charlie's boat, and it sank. I was afraid he was going to be really mad at me. Well, I knew where to find him. I called the Occidental Bar where he was and told him his boat had sunk. 'Oh, that's okay,' he said, 'don't worry about it. It needs a good douching now and then, anyway.' He came back the next day, and he and Adam Greenwald drug it up on the beach. It had a little four-banger Grey Marine in it. He and Adam had it purring like a kitten a couple days later. Three days after it sank, he was going fishing. He was tougher than hell. He was a good guy, friendly, sit around telling stories, you know. I miss those old-timers. That was before we had television and telephones. We'd just sit around and have a few beers and tell stories."

"Yeah," said Kenny, "they used to call it the Accidental bar. It was one of the old-timers' favorite hangouts.

"You know who else used to hang out there was ol' Tubbs. Now that guy was full of it. He was a good shipwright, but he was one hell of a storyteller."

"Yeah," said Floyd, "he was telling me a story of being out in a submarine off the Aleutian Islands patrolling for Japs during the war. He says, 'We dove so deep that when we finally came to the surface our eyes popped out, just like a red snapper!' So I said, 'Well, what did you do, Charlie?' 'We just shoved them back in,' he said. 'They fit right back into the sockets.'"

The Greybeards

Needless to say, that set off an explosive round of laughter from everyone gathered there.

For reasons I can't remember, I had to leave shortly thereafter, but I knew then that I had to at least attempt to capture some of the history of the fishermen who have chosen fishing as a career and Hoonah as a home. This book isn't politically correct. Some people may take offense at the language or phrases used, but wherever possible, I've quoted the fishermen. An attempt to change the jargon would be akin to modifying the character of the person speaking; it would be almost blasphemous. I can't attest to the factual content of what has been spoken by these anglers, but I think that the stories they've told are etched in their memories as they remember them, and as far as they are concerned, they are true.

Windy Skaflestad

Few things are more embarrassing for a commercial fisherman than pulling up to the cold storage dock with a small load of fish. I've been selling to the local fish processing plant, Hoonah Cold Storage, for 30-some years, so they know not to expect too much from me. Nonetheless, it's frustrating when the guys you've been fishing around, some of whom aren't known for being especially good fishermen, double or triple your score. When that happens, I always like to make it sound like I wasn't really trying that hard or I'd only put in a few hours to see if there were any fish around. I've been known to

The Greybeards

come in and sell at the end of the day when everyone else has returned to his stall and I don't have an audience to witness my miserable tally. Even then, I've had dock workers look over the side of the bull rail and seeing just a few fish in the bucket ask, "Is that all?" To say the least, it's humbling. I don't know why it bothers me so much. It's not like I have a great reputation as a highliner that I have to defend. On the contrary, it's always a surprise to everyone when I do show up with a good load. This past spring, the king salmon fishing was especially slow around the Icy Strait area. When I happened to catch four kings in one day, it was the talk of the dock. No one was more surprised than me, though.

In my quest to gain some useful tidbit that will help me in my chosen profession, I thought I would ask some of the folks who have been doing this for years to share their stories. Fishing stories are never just about fishing. There is usually a geography or history lesson thrown into the mix. Sometimes there's a little physics involved or gossip, and sometimes it's just plain common sense, but I welcome it all. I figure the more I know, the better my chances of being successful.

I spend a good bit of time every year fishing in and around Port Frederick, the bay in front of Hoonah where I live. It's close by, and usually when Icy Strait is too rough to fish, I can still drag my hooks inside the bay and at least put in an effort.

When the Huna Tlingit were driven out of their homes in Glacier Bay by the advancing glaciers, they traveled to

Windy Skaflestad

various points in Icy Strait looking for a suitable place to establish a new village. They finally opted for Brown Bear Bay, as Port Frederick was known prior to the arrival of white settlers. According to the elders, the bay was also known for a time as Ku S'eil after a female slave named S'eil who was sacrificed there. By whatever name it is called, the bay has provided an abundant living for the residents of the area since the first people arrived.

In my opinion, no one knows Port Frederick better than the Skaflestad family. They've been logging and fishing the area for longer than I've been alive, so Windy Skaflestad was one of the first people I spoke to. He's given me tips in the past, so I was eager to glean a little more from his storehouse of knowledge, but perhaps even more, I was hoping to get some insight into how Hoonah and the fishing fleet have changed through the years.

I visited Windy at his home on Lumbago Way, a winding gravel road that parallels the mudflats that stretch toward the airport. It was February, and the ground outside was frozen solid. The wind was whipping ghostlike threads of snow across the barren landscape where it would lodge in small drifts against an assortment of buildings and vehicles around the compound; inside, though, it was toasty warm.

Windy motioned for me to take a chair and sat down across from me. We engaged in some small talk — the cold weather, his health and some of the plans he's working on as mayor of Hoonah.

When I asked about some of the changes he's seen in

The Greybeards

his 70-some years, he shifted in his chair and pointed to the east, in the direction of the Icy Strait Lodge, the local hotel.

"About where the lodge is now was a shipwright's building. It was a big building, owned by Silas Dalton. He was related to the Hubbard family."

And so my education began. He proceeded to point out another handful of spots along the beach where other shipwrights had built ways and shops for hauling boats in and out of the tidal flats and repairing them. In the early days, wood boats ruled supreme, and shipwrights were as common as seagulls wherever men made a living from the sea. At one time there were a number of small fishermen's cabins located along Lumbago Way. The cabins are gone now, as well as the fishermen who owned them. All that remains of the ways are a few logs rotting on the flats. As an owner of a wooden boat, I wish that the shops were still around.

"A lot of the trollers started here," he said. "The first trollers just fished out of wooden skiffs. They rowed around with a little crotched stick that they stuck in the back oarlock chocks, and then that went up to their other set of oars and a leather went around their wrist and back to the cotton line, so that when they were rowing, the lure moved with the oars. That's all they used when I was a little kid. Then they used what they called a football lead. You don't see those anymore, either. There were all different weights on those. I think they used 5 pound for hand trolling."

Windy Skaflestad

Hand trollers had no mechanical propulsion and manually pulled aboard all the fish they caught. By 1913, though, power trollers were coming on the scene. Apparently government fishery managers didn't care for them initially; they feared too many salmon would be lost because they trolled too fast, and it was felt that they couldn't play the fish. There was a feeling at the time that hand trolling was an option for people with a limited amount of money, and thus anyone could get into it, providing employment in an area where work wasn't always readily available. Only 34 power troll permits were issued that year, as opposed to 389 hand troll permits. Twelve years later, however, power trollers accounted for the bulk of the salmon caught. Eventually all trollers were motorized, though hand trollers are still limited to manually pulling their gear.

"The first power troll operations were pretty primitive," Windy commented. "Back in those days, they had a model A or T transmission box with chains on it and it connected to pulleys in the back, and that's what they ran their gurdies with. Nothing was covered, everything was exposed. Back in those days, you didn't have OSHA (Occupational Safety and Health Administration) breathing down your neck. You slapped on plenty of grease on the moving parts, and everything just kept working. Of course, when you got home you looked like a grease job."

Though the modern troll fleet ranges far and wide in pursuit of its quarry, in the early years many of the local

The Greybeards

trollers confined their fishing to areas around Icy Strait — Point Adolphus, Pleasant Island, Homeshore, Spasski, Whitestone Harbor and Point Sophia. Apparently it was common for the various tenders to assist the hand trollers by towing their skiffs out to the fishing grounds. Ten to 12 skiffs would be bobbing in the wake of the tender, like ducklings following their mother. From Hoonah to Point Adolphus to the west was a distance of roughly 15 miles. Whitestone Harbor was a few miles farther if they turned to the east. Because of the great distance, travel to and from town wasn't practical, so they set up troller's camps — tents pitched close to a freshwater stream. They would anchor their skiffs off the beach, and every two or three days a tender would pass by to pick up their catch and run the fish into Juneau for processing. Today fishermen have a number of options for selling their catch. There are processors located up and down the coast with most sending out tenders or buying scows where the fisherman can sell his catch. Boats with a small hold have the option of selling every day and replenishing their supply of ice and groceries. Larger boats can hold fish for up to five days before they have to sell, while freezer boats process their catch on board and frequently don't return to port until the hold is full. Unless you have a freezer boat, ice is always a consideration for a troller. The flesh of fish will break down rapidly if it's not maintained at a relatively cold temperature. I asked Windy how they dealt with this issue.

"The buyers usually came either every day or every

Windy Skaflestad

other day," he responded. "When the fish buyer showed up, the boats would stop fishing and go sell their fish. We could hold our fish for three days."

"You didn't have ice, though?"

"No, we had to keep them covered with burlap and with water on them. Yep, they'd hold pretty good for three days; in fact, they were better than a lot of fish that I've seen come over the dock, but the first thing you had to do was gut them."

Prior to my arrival in the mid-70s, icebergs were a common sight in the area around Icy Strait. For years there was no ice commercially available in Hoonah, so the halibut boats would come alongside the bergs and chip it off. They had to exercise caution, though. With so much of the ice under the water, taking too much off of one side could cause the berg to flip and damage the vessel. Occasionally the icebergs made their way up into Garteeni Creek, which parallels the airport runway. At the time there was no breakwater to prevent them from floating up on the tide.

Windy was still in grade school when his uncle, Don Underwood, took him out trolling for the first time.

"I don't know what year it was, it was in the 40s. They were rebuilding Hoonah after the fire. (Much of Hoonah was destroyed by a fire on June 14, 1944.) My uncle was running the restaurant for the contractors behind the school. Anyhow, he bought me a bamboo pole with an Ocean City reel on it. We went up fishing where the log dump is. I caught my first fish there. I had a slip sinker on

The Greybeards

the line, and that coho hit and started jumping, and we lost the sinker. My uncle had a pocket watch that he tied on for a weight, and we fished the rest of the day with that. When he got home, he just washed it out and put it in alcohol and dried it, and it worked!"

Evidently that first coho was the spark that lit the desire to fish in Windy, and he's been fishing ever since. First with rods, then hand gurdies and now power gear. He turned and pointed to a picture on the wall. It was an 8x10 black and white photo that showed somewhere between 25 and 30 huge king salmon gutted and lying on the snow.

"That was one day's fishing — rod and reel. Look at how big they are. There's a lot of them 40 pounds and better."

Though he didn't say, I think it was a combined effort of him and possibly one or two of his brothers. Fishing has been a way of life for his family for years.

He turned back to me and commented, "That just shows you the kind of fishing we had around here. The bay is crazy. I've seen it right at the point in the Narrows going in … you couldn't keep them off your line. You couldn't fish with two rods. You'd skip a herring across the top and *wham*, you had one. Those fish were like that all the way up to the head of the bay. There was times when the herring were just boiling. Especially up in Eight Fathom Bight — that was just a mass of herring. We were logging at Seagull Flats one year, and here come the herring seiners from Petersburg and Sitka, and there

Windy Skaflestad

might have been some from some other places, but they seined from Neka Bay all the way up to Midway Island. They may have gone farther up — we couldn't see because we were working — but they seined those herring, and ever since those years the herring has never come back."

Without the herring to attract them into the bay, the king salmon now just seem to pass through sporadically. There are times when there might be a day or two of relatively good king fishing, but in my 32 years of fishing Port Frederick, I've never seen anything to compare with what I saw in that picture.

"We had a camp up in Salt Chuck," he said, "just past where the forest service float is now, and the old man had a 10-foot fiberglass skiff with a Martin outboard on it … ran like hell. Anyway, he started down the bay, and he got just to the sandy point by Hillman's Ranch in the bight there and the king salmon were just chasing herring. Well, he had a piece of string and an old tarnished Superior spoon laying in the bottom of the boat that he tied on and gave it a heave, and *bang* — he got quite a few on that. We couldn't believe it. You don't see that in the bay anymore. You probably could, but no one spends the time up there like we used to. We were up there 24 hours a day, seven days a week. We didn't come to town too often."

While he was growing up, Windy and his brothers fished in the winter, but summers were reserved for working with their father, Alf, on his logging operation. He had a contract with Excursion Inlet Packing Company to provide logs for pilings and floating fish traps.

The Greybeards

Prior to Alaska becoming a state in 1959, the federal government had control over the territorial fisheries. During that time, fish traps were placed at multiple points along Icy Strait. According to Windy, there were traps on either side of Spasski Bay, Point Sophia, Eagle Point, Pinta Cove and the back side of Point Adolphus.

One trap, located at Point Gustavus at the entrance to Glacier Bay, had to be rebuilt every year because the icebergs that drifted out of the bay destroyed it. After Alaska obtained statehood, fish traps were outlawed, a move that many say saved the salmon fishery in Southeast Alaska.

So often when I'm out fishing, I'm aware that my fellow fishermen are pulling many times more fish than me. It's incredibly frustrating, so I thought I would see if Windy could shed any light on the problem.

"Why do some guys get so many fish?" I asked.

"They just, uh, they just — I don't know. I don't know what it is. Fish are funny. That orange boat I had would out-fish the one I have now. I just had two lines then, but I'd catch more fish with less gear. I'd be fishing the same gear as Gus (his son) was fishing, when Gus was fishing the *Wolf*. We'd go out there together, and Gus would pull twice as much fish as me. Same gear. Same speed. There's just something about it."

While that wasn't the answer I was searching for, I felt that at least it was an honest one. There is a saying that 20 percent of the fishermen catch 80 percent of the fish. That may be fairly accurate. No doubt there is a good deal of

Windy Skaflestad

skill involved, but often I think it's a matter of putting in your time and being where the fish are.

Among the many changes that have taken place through the years is the shrinking of the commercial fishing fleet. In the early 1970s the troll fleet was pared down by limiting individuals who had a documented history of commercial trolling. While many of the Hoonah locals had fished off and on through the years, either as crew hands or on their own boats, they lacked the documentation necessary to qualify for a limited entry permit. The seine fleet as well was reduced by the closure of Inian Pass to the seiners. The local areas that remained open could no longer sustain a large seine fleet. Though there are still a few local seine boats here, the once proud Hoonah seine fleet is a thing of the past.

In contrast, where the commercial fleet once dominated the fisheries, more and more sport charter boats have shown up on the scene. In 2003 Hoonah became a port of call for the cruise ship industry, and ever since that time the number of charter boats has been on the increase. Local residents aren't the only ones to take the tourists fishing. A number of Juneau boats now come into the Icy Strait area to fish, as well as boats from lodges located in Gustavus and Excursion Inlet. It feels to me like an invasion, and it's something I don't deal with very well.

In addition to the charter boats, there are a rising number of retirees who've found Hoonah to be to their liking. They've wintered their boats in the harbor and spend their summers taking friends from the lower 48 out

The Greybeards

for a day's fishing. The harbor is littered with their Dungeness crab pots, and periodically pots are placed in the high traffic areas, causing some ill will toward the owners.

Over the past five or six years there has been a fleet of Canadian sport fishermen who spend a week or two fishing the area. For the most part they are a friendly enough lot, but they're not here to just catch a few fish and have fun — they've come to fill their freezers for the winter with Alaskan halibut and salmon. It's a sore subject with many of us as we wonder how many pounds of fish a person needs and speculation about the illegal sale or bartering of sport-caught fish is tossed around.

To add fuel to the fire, several years ago the federal government instituted a statute allowing the smaller coastal towns to harvest subsistence halibut. While I have no issue with that, they permit a maximum of 30 hooks to be run with a limit of 20 halibut per day. That's a lot of fish in anyone's book. The very entity that is charged with protecting the resource has opened the possibility of overfishing under the guise of subsistence. Once again, common sense has taken a back seat to political correctness, and the resource we rely on will suffer as a result.

For years sea lions and sea otters were fair game to fishermen. They are both known for their voracious appetites. Adult sea lions eat hundreds of pounds of fish every day and frequently follow the trollers and take fish right off their hooks. I spoke to one native fellow who

Windy Skaflestad

claimed that the natives never let a sea lion come through Inian Pass. They killed any that they found, knowing full well the damage that they could do to the fishery. Now such an act will land a person in jail with a stiff fine to boot. It's more evidence of just how the times have changed. The locals curse the sea otters for wiping out the abalone. Otters also have a fondness for clams, as well as crabs. I've heard a number of people say they will destroy a clam bed, harvesting clams until it's as barren as a desert, then move on to a new area. I mentioned this to Windy.

"They worry about the whales and sea lions and whatnot nowadays, but, Tom, when I was growing up, just getting started in fishing, the fleet used to congregate at Adolphus and over at Homeshore. There must have been a couple hundred boats — trollers and seiners — nothing but masts sticking up everywhere. Now they're worried about a single boat going by. We had whales back then; we had sea lions back then — they're nothing new. They're new to the tourists, they never seen them before. A lot of these charter guys are young; they're not from around here, so it's all new to them."

Indeed, an entire industry has sprung up taking tourists out to Point Adolphus to see the Humpback whales and other wildlife that congregates there to feed on the abundance of krill and herring. There are a number of businesses that have flourished because of the tourists' interest in seeing the otters, seals and sea lions. Of course, there is no mention of the destructive habits that some of these creatures have. Everything in the ocean feeds on

The Greybeards

something else, but to the paying public, they are portrayed as cute.

"Nowadays they talk about conservation; we have some reel-to-reel footage that my dad took years ago, and it will show you my grandmother with us up in the camp with her smokehouse. Us kids were the ones who would go get the dog salmon for her. All the rivers were different for texture of the meat. She preferred the fish from Bell Island River, on the right-hand side, up in the head of the bay. That was the coldest river. We used to go up there and she would say, 'Okay, I only want five,' and we did not dare catch more or damage any of them. Mom and her would go out and dig clams. She had an 18-foot flat-bottom homemade boat, a nice skiff, and she would take it out on a minus tide and let it go dry on the flats. Then we would load it about half full of clams, and when the tide came back in, it would float all the way back to the camp. She would sit there and clean every clam — you didn't throw nothing away. The old-timers didn't let nothing spoil. They ate the fish eggs and the heads. They'd ferment the heads."

I had heard of the practice of fermenting the heads and eggs in what was commonly known as stink heads or stink eggs. Windy let me know that he didn't partake of any. I, too, have been offered the eggs but declined.

"The bay has been quite a provider." He sighed. "This bay has pretty much been our life for 71 years, and we pretty well know it, though sometimes we pretend like we don't," he said, smiling. "We kind of sneak the other

Windy Skaflestad

fishermen up on the rocks. Yeah, over the years, the bay was pretty exciting. It's a hell of a change, but I'm glad I'm still here to remember what went on."

Like all of us, time has taken a toll on Windy, and he doesn't get out fishing as much as he used to or would like to. As of this writing, he's doing his second stint as mayor of our fair city, so that may restrict his fishing time even more. He's also battling some health issues, but I'm sure that when the spring winds blow fair and word of a king salmon run reaches his ears, he'll fire up the engines on the *Legal Tender* and come grab his share of the bounty, just as he's done for years.

Jim Dybdahl

Mention the name Jim Dybdahl almost anywhere that fishermen gather in Southeast Alaska and you're sure to find at least a few people who are familiar with the man and his boat, the *Coronation*. He's traveled from Warren Island in the south to Yakutat in the north and every bay and passage in between in search of his quarry.

Over the years Jim has developed the reputation of being a great fisherman with a great product. He has a loyal customer base in Juneau that look forward to a call or e-mail stating that he's in town with some fresh salmon or halibut for sale. People line up to fork over their hard-

Jim Dybdahl

earned money for a chance to take home some premium Alaskan seafood. The professionalism he brings to the industry is an asset that we all benefit from as fishermen and as consumers as well.

Jim first caught the fishing bug back in 1965 when he was 10 years old. He was visiting his dad, Paul Dybdahl Sr., captain of the *Point Sophia*, a 70-foot tender docked at the Hoonah cannery. The cook aboard the boat asked young Jim if he would be interested in rowing the little 8-foot pram that was stored topside. They launched the small skiff, and after paddling around in front of the cannery dock for a while, the cook waved him over. He had a rod and reel in his hand and said, "Being as how you're out here going back and forth, you may as well try and catch a fish." The rest, as they say, is history.

"He baited up a hook for me with herring and sent me out, and not even 10 minutes later, I nailed a king salmon, a 21-pound white," Jim said. "I'll always remember that because when I got it close to the boat, the cook was yelling, 'Do you have something to club it with?'

"Well, there was nothing in the boat, so he went down to the seine boats that were moored there and ran from boat to boat looking for something to use as a gaff. No one had anything, so he grabbed a 2x4 and ran out in the power skiff and came alongside of me and whacked the fish with the board and reached under the gill plate and lifted the king aboard. We went back aboard the *Point Sophia*, and everybody from the cannery came to the top of the dock to look at the kid and his catch. After that

The Greybeards

finally faded off, the cook said, 'Well, gosh, you've got to go do it again.' So I baited up and started rowing again, and by the last point at the cannery where the dolphins are, I'll be doggone if I didn't get another one. This time I had a gaff hook aboard; I got one from my dad's boat. I landed that one — it was an 18 pounder. I went back again, baited up and got a 12 pounder, right in front of the cannery houses. I had three kings in about an hour's time. My dad came up to the house here where my mom lived and said, 'We got to get this kid out fishing, so here's what we'll do; you and Jim can take my 14-foot plywood skiff out (it had a 10-horse Evinrude outboard on it) and go out and fish by Point Sophia. I'll sell your fish for you, and when you make enough money, we'll buy you your own commercial license.' At that time all it was, was $35 for a troll license.

"Interestingly enough, I remember the coho price back then — it was 35 cents a pound. We used to have one of those oval galvanized tubs in the front of our skiff. If we could fill that up with 33 fish, it would usually average about $100, but we hardly ever got that. As a matter of fact, it took us about five days to get the 35 bucks. It was early July so there weren't that many cohos around, mostly humpies. Anyway, we got our license and started venturing out to the wild blue yonder, which was Hoonah Island and Flynn Cove, and that was about our range that year. There were about three or four other skiffs, including Adam Greenwald and old Jim Austin Sr. They all knew which boat my mother and I had and looked out for us.

Jim Dybdahl

"The first year I got 10 percent of the earnings and the second year I got 15 percent, and then we got a nice fiberglass boat with a 33-horsepower Evinrude. Actually it started out with a 33, but it was too hard for me to start; I was too small at the time, so we traded it in for a 25-horse Johnson. Then we started making some journeys, to like Pleasant Island and Porpoise Island. My mom had a determination to make at least $20 every day, so we had to stay out no matter what. If it was rough, we would fish by Cannery Point and out toward Point Sophia, and we had to make that 20 bucks in order for her to want to go in. That took about six cohos. I soon learned that it would be better for me to get good at baiting and when we got the six cohos, quit. I remember a lot of times when we'd get out fishing, I'd bait up the two lines we had and put them in the water, and I'd go back to sleep on the seat. My mom would just sit there and troll back and forth. Sometimes she would see the strike, and sometimes she wouldn't. At the time, the first couple of years, we didn't have Pink Ladies (diving planes); we just had half-moon leads and bait. The fish would hit hard enough to ruin the bait, but not hard enough to get caught, so if the bait got struck and got ruined, we were towing around a bad bait for however long she let me sleep. Sometimes it would be an hour, and then she'd say, 'Jim, you've got to get up and check the bait,' and sure enough I'd change the bait and we'd start getting strikes."

Growing up, Jim's favorite places to fish were Black Rock or Noon Point on Pleasant Island, though his

The Greybeards

mother preferred fishing along the shore leading out to Point Adolphus. Though they were in a rather small boat, they never had to spend the night out due to bad weather.

"My mother had a theory that if you just took it slow you could make it through even the rough stuff, which was true. If you just slowed the boat down you might be rocking back and forth, but you weren't plunging off the wave too fast."

Talking to Jim, I wished that I could have gone fishing with him and his mom. Unlike me, she didn't show any sign of being afraid of the weather, and because she wasn't, Jim didn't recall experiencing any anxiety over it.

"She was pretty steadfast at steering the boat. There were times when it was raining where I would be peeking out underneath my rain hood, hunkered down on the seat waiting for a fish to bite, and she'd be sitting there. She had one of those plastic rain bonnets tied around her chin, and I remember the rain just beating off her face and she'd just be looking ahead — she loved it out there.

"She fished with me for five years, and then when I was 15, I told her that I was ready to go by myself. Although she hated to stop going, she let me go. Two or three years later she remarried and ended up with a little Hi-Laker. There were actually two ladies who were pretty well known for trolling at the time. One was my mother, and the other was Rosie Stevenson. Ol' Rosie was a hard-nosed dragger. She spent all of her time on this shore over here, on the Spasski shore and whatnot."

With all the talk of global warming and over fishing

Jim Dybdahl

and with the exploding number of lodges and commercial sport charter boats plying the waters of Icy Strait, I wondered if Jim has seen a decline in the number of fish now, compared to when he was young.

"I believe there was probably more fish on the inside … I think there's the same amount of fish, but there's more pressure out there on the ocean coast, and it takes longer for the fish to boil over into here. We didn't catch huge amounts, even as I got better as a junior or senior in high school. I think the best day I ever had with rod and reels was 97 cohos, over at Groundhog Bay. I ran out of bait at noon. I was using herring fillets and a Pink Lady at that time, and luckily I saved all the backbones in a bucket because I believed you didn't want to feed all the fish, make them fill up on your discards. When I ran out of bait at noon, I think I had 50 cohos, and I started using heads and backbones and tails, and I caught another 47 when I quit at 5:00. I had three rods at the time, and I was pulling fairly steady. I'd pull 10, 12 fish and then I'd clean them and start the process all over again.

"I had boxes for the fish in the skiff, and I covered them with burlap to keep them cool. When I filled up my boxes, I put them in the back in the trough there where the engines are and covered them with kelp. When it came time to leave, it took me about two miles to get that boat up on step. I was leaning up on the bow, up over the windshield, because it was so heavy. It was fun, and there was nobody else there. I just stumbled on them. Danny Neal was fishing over by Spasski, and he had a fairly good

The Greybeards

day, 50, 60 fish there, but I pulled up with my 97, and needless to say, Danny beat me back to my spot there the next morning.

"We used to buy our bait right here at Hoonah Seafoods or down at the cold storage. Whenever they ran out of Tom Brown's bait, we used to buy boxes of bulk herring; we were just using it for fillets. You could use the last third or last half of a big herring and make a nice fillet out of it. I didn't like to use fresh herring because they were soft. I always filleted my herring first thing in the morning after I ran out (to the fishing grounds). I'd take out four or five dozen herring, and I would sit there and fillet herring for about an hour and put them in a bucket so that when the bite came I was ready."

"Did you use a Les Davis Herring Aid?" I asked. (Herring Aids imparted a rolling motion to the bait.)

"No, just two hooks, solid tie. I had a method of baiting them. The cut on this fillet and the method of hooking them up was taught to us by our dad. I'm not sure who he learned it from, but my older brother, Johan, taught it to me. It was a big secret. Almost nobody else used fillets like we did, and we were a lot more successful for the most part than a lot of the guys here. So they were always trying to figure out … as a matter of fact when I would tie up next to Danny Neal and we would share lunch, I used to turn my back to him and bait up my hook, hiding the secret baiting because I didn't want him to learn — it was my ace in the hole. My filleted bait would catch a lot more cohos while we were just drifting around

Jim Dybdahl

than his whole herring would. It would drive him nuts. In fact, I would catch four or five to every one of his while we were having lunch together. He knew it was a fillet, but he didn't know how it was hooked or how it was cut. Then one year there was a bait company called Tyee that supplied the bait for the stores, and lo and behold, on the back was a picture of my fillet and the correct way to hook it up. I don't know if anybody tried it or not; I never hinted to the fact that it was the exact blueprint. To this day, I don't see that many people using fillets like that. They either use one hook or a different configuration of hooking it up. Boy, at times, especially when the needlefish are present, a fillet will out-fish a whole herring just because it's thinner in size, more streamlined."

Given the fact that filleted herring worked so well for Jim in his rod fishing days, it would seem logical that he would use them for his power trolling, though I know it takes a lot longer to deal with bait, and unlike hoochies or spoons, the bait is only good for one fish. If it's damaged somehow, it will quit fishing. Then again, Jim is quite successful with whatever lure he uses, natural or man-made. I asked him about using bait for power trolling.

"No, I'm a lazy power troller. I should be baiting all the time for king salmon when it's slow. I had a lesson last year when I was down around Warren Island. Pat and Bonnie were fishing near me, and they were beating me by a handful or two of fish a day. Bonnie is a real avid fisherman, she really works the gear, and I know she likes to bait. I hadn't really been doing all that well, so they

The Greybeards

floated me some bait, and I baited up all my hooks. Well, I made one turn in the evening before I quit, and I caught 11 kings all at one time. They were all on bait. They went all around my spoons and all around my hoochies. It just reconfirmed what I've known all along, that I should be baiting more or being more ambitious. The really good fishermen are using a lot of bait."

Jim displays the quiet confidence of a professional who is sure of himself and his abilities and isn't afraid to share his knowledge with those of us who aren't so blessed. I wanted to make sure that I wasn't divulging any fishing secrets, and he assured me he had no secrets.

With his purchase of the *Coronation* back in 1988, he was no longer confined to the local areas, and now ranges far and wide in pursuit of his quarry. When asked if he had a favorite spot for dragging, he said, "I don't know if I have any favorite area. I cover a lot of territory. This last year alone I made five trips from Hoonah down to the lower end of Chatham and back. I can't even imagine how many miles I put under the keel last year, but it was considerable."

Chatham Strait is an incredibly long body of water in Southeast Alaska, stretching north and south for roughly 150 miles or so. Because it has such a long way to build, the winds can be ferocious, and the seas can build to dangerous levels. With that in mind, I wondered about the weather Jim encountered in his many travels.

"For the most part, as long as it doesn't get more than 25 knots, you can travel in that without any problem. I

Jim Dybdahl

won't fish in anything above 35, I don't think. One year, me and 26 other guys got caught out on the Fairweather Grounds. The forecast was for 20, 25 southeast, which was manageable, as long as you've got your gear in the water. You'll toss and turn, but it's fishable. I remember that it was the 5th of July. We woke up in the morning, and it had been a kind of bumpy night, it was blowing 25 southeast all night long. There's no place to anchor, you're 40 miles offshore. At night when it's time to shut down, I run about three-quarters to a mile away from the nearest boat, and you kind of judge the size of the boat that you're laying next to because the bigger boats will catch more wind and move faster. It's a huge area out there, miles and miles and miles, so you just find a spot. I don't worry about the cruise ships. They mainly run inside of the Fairweather Grounds. I don't know if it's because of the troll fleet or if they're trying to avoid the shallows, but there is a 13 fathom spot out there.

"Surprisingly there are a lot of fish out in the deep. You drag 30 to 50 fathoms of gear. You're just out there like a big columbine on an open field harvesting. You can travel five, 10, 20 miles sometimes in one direction. A couple of years ago when that big body of fish was up there, they figured that the body was about a mile wide by 35 miles long. That's a lot of fish. I just didn't happen to be there that year.

"Anyway, we got caught with that weather forecast thinking it was going to be 25, and we woke up in the morning and started fishing, and it was kind of miserable,

The Greybeards

but we started catching fish; we had a clatter of about 10 kings, so we thought, well, if we put in the day we might end up with 40 or 50 kings. Then about 10:00 we got a call from Pat on the *Seka*. He had left the day before because his son and Bonnie were feeling kind of bad. He was down off of Cape Fairweather. He said, 'Gee I can't believe you're still fishing — it's nasty here.' I just figured some people can take it and some can't. So I said, 'It's fishable here.'

"What I didn't realize at the time was that it really was nasty along the shoreline, that the blow hadn't come out off the shore yet. Pat said he was going to put it on his stern and run up to Yakutat; he was about 10 hours away from there. So he told me to be safe. I started noticing about one or two in the afternoon that the swells were getting close together, and they were getting fairly large. It was still blowing 25, but the swells were stacking up. It was getting kind of cruddy out there. I listened to the forecast at 4:00, and they were calling for 25, increasing to 30 and back down to 25 the next day. My son Donald and my nephew Torin were fishing with me and I told them, 'We're going to have to make a decision. It's cruddy right now, and if it blows five more knots and we have to drift in this tonight it's going to be flat nasty. The way it is right now we've got an 8- to 10-hour buck into this stuff to try and get back to Cape Spencer, and that's going to put us into the darkness, and I don't really want to be bucking into the darkness. The other option is to run into the shore and try to get into Lituya Bay; we'll get there at the

Jim Dybdahl

wrong time, and we'll have to wait until about 1 a.m. when the tide starts flooding. The thing is, as bad as it's looking now, we might get stuck in Lituya, and we're on our fifth day of trolling so we need to deliver on the sixth.'

"So, the obvious answer to me was to go with it and run to Yakutat so I could get rid of the fish. I calculated the run, and it was about 11 hours. Meanwhile Pat was just arriving in Yakutat, so I told him I would check in every hour.

"At 6:00 I calculated that I was 43 miles offshore and 67 miles from Ocean Cape, near Yakutat. At 7:00 it started getting considerably rougher, and I told Pat, 'Get a pen and paper; I'm going to start giving you actual latitude and longitude readings.' He said, 'Oh, boy. Oh, boy. It's getting bad, huh?' I said, 'Well, let's put it this way, I want you to tell those flyboys from the Coast Guard where my exact location was the last time you talked to me.'

"A double-ender (like the *Coronation*) running before a big swell like that is no fun. If you get it on the quarter stern, the boat really rolls, so I was trying to keep the boat running with the waves, yet I was having to angle whenever I could, because running with it would put me up at Point Mamby, on the other side of Yakutat Bay. I started looking at the tide book and the time I was going to arrive and whatnot. It was a big tide, about a 17, 18 footer on the inside, so I knew that tide was going to be outgoing, and I didn't want to be too far off Ocean Cape. If you get that much water coming out of the bay against a southeast, you're going to have big rips there, so I knew I had to be on that shoreline, so I kept trying to edge the boat over, but it just kept building on me.

"About 8:00 I got a call on the VHF from Wayne on the *Hoyden*. He had caught up with me, and his crew hand was on the afterdeck with a video camera; they got a little footage of me as they were coming up on me, and it's pretty spooky. Believe it or not, that wasn't all that bad, at that time, but the old *Coronation* was just corkscrewing. I looked out the back door, and it was just kind of frightening. I spent more time looking out my side window, trying to gauge when the swells weren't so big and I could cut across them at an angle, and when the big ones would come, I would put them directly on my stern.

"Wayne checked in on the sideband radio with Pat and me at 8:00, and I remember Pat pleading with Wayne not to leave me behind. He said, 'You don't know what a bad ride is until you're in a double-ender in a following sea like that. Stay with my buddy, Jim.' So Wayne agreed. Anyway, from 8:00 until midnight it was a steady 35, maybe 40, and running 8- to 12-foot seas, and we got into a flow. Things were going smooth enough that I turned the boat over to Donald. I told him, 'I've got to have some sleep. I only got about three hours of sleep last night, and I've been up since 3:00 this morning. We're not going to get into Yakutat until about 4 a.m., so I need to rest.'

"As it was, I could barely stay in the day bunk up topside. I actually started to doze off a little bit. It wasn't all that bad when you're on the bunk, but when I sat up to get ready to take over the wheel and looked out the back, it

Jim Dybdahl

was actually pretty frightening. I took over from Donald and I told him, 'Okay, go down below, and get Torin and get out your survival suits and get real familiar with them, 'cause it's going to be a long, long night.' It was definitely blowing 35 to 40, with 8- to 12-foot seas with an occasional 15 footer. It was totally off the forecast, so I didn't know what was coming. It wasn't bad. I got into a rhythm; there would be about two or three humongous waves and I would have to maneuver the boat so that it was directly stern to, and then as soon as they passed by me, I had to turn the boat 45 degrees to starboard to try and correct my course because I was getting pushed farther and farther off to the west. That was my whole program up until about midnight. Along about 1:30, Wayne's deckhand, Mary, called me and said, 'Jim, we got a problem; we've lost our steering.'"

Few things are worse than losing the ability to maneuver your boat in bad weather. As it was, though, Wayne had an idea of what the problem was and was able to fix it within 10 minutes. Jim slowed the *Coronation* down to about three knots to be of some support to his friends, though they all knew that in the rough seas towing the *Hoyden* wasn't going to be possible.

"While I was waiting to hear from Wayne, I noticed that the boat was starting to feel real unstable. I thought maybe it was because I was slowed down that I was losing my steerage. I talked to Mary on the *Hoyden* and told them that I would have to speed up, and she assured me that the problem was almost fixed, to go ahead.

The Greybeards

"About 10 minutes later, Pat called me for the 2 a.m. check-in. While I was talking to him, I looked out the side of my window, and all I saw was black. I had been able to see the tops of waves and frothy white and whatnot, but all of a sudden, it was black, and I knew what that was — it was a big wave right next to me. I don't know if it was a combination of me getting distracted while I was talking on the radio or if it was just a freak thing, but I felt the boat rising on this wave. It didn't crash over the boat, but it caught the *Coronation* on its side and just kept shoving me and shoving me, sideways. As the wave passed by, it was moving so quickly that I found myself in the trough, and the boat was leaning way over; all of a sudden, the boat was on its side and just stayed there. Everything started falling from the starboard side of the boat to the port side. I couldn't believe it! I'm on the radio talking to Pat, and someone starts screaming, 'We're going over!' I was yelling at them to get on their survival suits, and the bilge alarm was going off because we were taking water in through the cockpit, and things were just crashing. I had just given my lat and long to Pat. I remember Wayne screaming, 'Where are you? Where are you?' and I'm trying to yell back at him.

"Of course, everyone is trying to push the button at the same time, and if you're transmitting, you can't receive, so there was pandemonium going on there. Finally I told Pat, 'I think I gotta go, I gotta go,' and I was reading my last position off to Wayne, when I felt the boat starting to right itself a little.

Jim Dybdahl

"I told Pat, 'Gosh, I think maybe it's coming back,' and I told the boys, 'Just wait, don't go yet (they were ready to launch the life raft). I'm going to turn the boat into the swell or turn the port side,' which was leaning way over at that point, I imagine, 45 or 50 degrees. Like I said, at one time I was flat on my side, virtually walking on the cabin walls on the port side. I was able to get the boat coming around, and it was slowly coming up, but by then I was getting bashed by the next set of 8- and 10-foot waves after that big one, so it took quite a while to get the port side to the waves and wind. Then amazingly I started swinging completely up and almost over to the starboard side, and I couldn't understand what the heck was going on.

"Wayne in the meantime was screaming on the VHF, 'Where are you, where are you? I can't see you! Turn on your strobe light!' I'm trying to manage the boat, the bilge alarm is just going constantly, things are crashing around and my two deckhands are totally freaked. I can't understand what's going on, so I was yelling at Donald, 'Did we lose our mast? Did the hayrack come off? Something is causing this boat to be totally unstable.' He tried to get out the door, and he couldn't, so I turned on the deck lights, and I tried to get out the door, but it felt like something was restricting it. I looked out the back window to see if something on the deck had moved in front of the door and there was nothing, and that's when I realized it was the force of the wind holding it closed. Then I understood that I was in a squall. It must have been blowing 70.

The Greybeards

"I finally comprehended that because of the storm, the *Hoyden* was now in front of me by a mile and a half or so, and while he was heading toward Ocean Cape, I was going to the west, and we were getting farther apart. At one point Wayne, who was closer in to shore and out of the squall, called on the VHF and said, 'I don't know what you're talking about, 70 mile an hour winds and 15- to 20-foot seas. It's blowing maybe 30 here, with 8- to 10-foot seas.' I said, 'Wayne, I don't know where you are, but I'm in hell!'

"I got the boat to the point that I was taking the waves on the starboard bow and was managing. The bilge pump finally caught up with the water that flooded the boat, and the alarm went off. We still had a fairly heavy list to the port from everything that had fallen from the starboard side, so I had my son check the fish hold to make sure the bin boards hadn't moved and allowed the fish to shift. He came back and said everything was fine down below; the poles were fine, and the mast was fine.

"I kept on this course, which actually put me heading back toward Cape Fairweather, Lituya Bay, and when Wayne finally calculated my position on his plotter, he said, 'Gosh, you're off behind me a ways. I'm coming.' We started talking about the difference in weather and our locations, and he said, 'I don't understand what you're talking about, Jim, it's not that rough.' As he got closer to my position, he started getting into the edge of that squall, and by the time he was close, he was into 10-, 12-foot waves, and it was blowing 50 where he was at. He finally called when he could see me and said, 'How come I'm looking at your green light? Where are you going?' I said, 'The boat is afloat at this course and this position, and I'm not going to change course until we hit the beach, and if that's Cape Fairweather, so be it.'

"He said, 'Okay, okay. We'll go this together.' Within 10 or 15 minutes, I made enough distance where I got out of that squall, and within a half hour it was blowing 25 easterly, and the waves were down to six or eight feet. So I turned my course for Ocean Cape, and it started getting daylight and got nicer and nicer as we got closer to shore. By the time we were three or four miles off the shore, it was almost calm. I remember just before we got into Ocean Cape, I looked at the screen and there were these great big balls of herring and feed, and I said, 'Gee, Wayne, look at all the feed on the screen.' Then Pat came on the radio and said, 'You goddamn Norwegian, you get your ass in here. We've been crying all night on your behalf. You get in here right now!'

"When I came around the cape, it was flat calm. I remember telling my son and nephew, 'Don't let me fall asleep now.' After all that adrenalin, my body was totally exhausted. I had a hard time staying awake for the last mile and a half to the anchorage. We got anchored up about 4:45, and it took us more than an hour to clean up the mess enough so we could lie on our bunks. There were things I hadn't seen for 10 years on that boat laying in the middle of the floor. They had come out of the cubbyholes and cupboards.

The Greybeards

"There were boats anchored up all around me that had been out on the West Bank the night before, and they were still straggling in by late morning. There were a lot of broken antenna masts and guys that lost their stabilizers and cables and took big thrashings, too. In fact, the *Avalon* was out there that night, and he almost sank; he got smacked by a wave that knocked his cabin back and damaged his poop deck. I think the Coast Guard helicopter was dropping him pumps at the same time I was in trouble. It was a frightening night for even the biggest boats. I'm sure the pucker factor was pretty high.

"It was just one of those freak storms. Maybe if we had been off the bank in deeper water it wouldn't have been so bad. It's a hard call. The Fairweather Grounds are notorious for their weather, but most of the weather stories are from when guys used to fish out there in earlier years, when you could fish out there in April, May or June. There hasn't been a major blow like that in the summer for a long time."

Such an ordeal would cause many people to consider fishing closer to home or perhaps even search out a less perilous vocation, but not Jim.

"Donald and I went out again the next year. The weather was good, and like they say, you fall off the horse, you've got to get back on, otherwise stay away from the horses. You know, fishing is my life, and we got a good report from out there, and we weren't doing so well where we were, so we made a decision to go back. We got out to the West Bank about four or five in the afternoon; it was

Jim Dybdahl

flat calm on the lower end and only one other boat there, off in the distance. We started catching fish, and from the time we arrived until dark, Donald and I caught 65 kings. I remember looking over and here's my son, working side by side with me, cleaning fish like crazy, and I looked up and all six lines were just hammering. I thought, *This is what it's all about.* We had a good time, and we got enough fish the next day on the morning bite to use up all the ice that we had available. In that short time, we had 130 kings, and we had to go."

The day was wearing on, and I'd already had several cups of Jim's coffee and used his bathroom once; before the urge struck again, I figured I'd better wrap up the interview.

"What do you anticipate for the future?" I asked.

"Well, as we get older the aches and pains are more prevalent, and I don't want to be making these 100-mile runs forever. If I can stay closer to home and grind out an average day, but get a high price for my fish, it will probably average out; and if I can get to the point where I can become a local processor, where I could buy fish from the local guys here and make sure those guys are meeting my standards on quality, and turn around and market those fish, they would get a better price, and it would be a win/win situation. But, you know, there is a lot of paperwork involved and a lot of time spent. On the other hand, if I can develop something along those lines and bring in some of my family and friends, then all I have to do is oversee. There are other options as far as my fishing,

The Greybeards

but it boils down to having a high quality product. I'm still considering buying a freezer boat. I have a friend who freezes who did quite well on his product this past year. The good thing about a freezer boat is you just stay out there until you're full. You're not running around like a crazy man every four to five days looking for a buyer for your fish. I have a young daughter who is pretty energetic who would make a wonderful crew hand, and my wife has always wanted to be part of this business, so it would be a mom and pop operation. We'll see how it goes."

Whatever the future holds for Jim, I'm sure it will involve fish, and I'm equally certain that it will be a success.

Jake White

Since my arrival in Alaska back in 1976, the only fishing I have been exposed to has been hook and line. Whether casting a spoon for Dolly Varden in one of the local streams or dragging a 50-pound cannonball behind a troller for salmon, I've never had the experience of fishing with a net. I don't even use one to bring the salmon I catch aboard, although there have been times when I knocked a nice salmon off the hook with a poorly placed swing of the gaff. Then I wish like heck that I had a net handy. However, because nets have a tendency to take the scales off the fish as they thrash around in it, and since the fish I

The Greybeards

sell are going to a market where appearance is important, I don't use one.

Because I'm unfamiliar with the seine fleet, which does use nets, most of the interviews I've done have been with the hook and line fishermen, like myself. Nevertheless, Hoonah has long had a number of captains and crew who have made their living aboard a seine boat, and in the interest of fairness and balance, I asked my neighbor, Jake White, if he would share a little bit of his knowledge with me. He owns the 58-foot seine boat *Mermaid*, a sharp-looking white seiner with turquoise trim.

We sat down at his kitchen table and started talking. Or at least I did.

At 80, he's one of the older fellows I've spoken to. Jake is Tlingit, the aboriginal people who reside in this region of Alaska. As is somewhat typical of the men his age and cultural background, he spoke sparingly at first, answering my questions with a single word or brief sentences. I was afraid the interview was going to be exceptionally short and somewhat difficult if I had to pry the answers from him.

"How old are you, Jake?"

"Eighty."

"Were you born here in Hoonah?" I asked.

"Sitka," he replied. "We lived there about nine years. My grandfather lived here, Archie White. He was too old to get wood or food, so we moved over here and stayed."

"How long have you had the *Mermaid*?"

"I don't know."

Jake White

"Did you have another boat before that one?"

"No."

"Are you still fishing?"

"No."

After a few minutes, he finally opened up.

"When was the last time you fished?" I asked.

"The doctor retired me," he said. "Gee, I had my crew … you know, I gave advance money to all my crew." He laughed. "I was going to beef up my seine. The doctor said something was wrong with my heart."

According to Jake, he has been fishing since he could walk. His father, Captain Joe White, was a fisherman and apparently a very good one. Jake turned in his chair and pointed to a picture on the wall. It was a black and white photo of a native man in a billed cap. I couldn't determine where or when it was taken, but it appeared to have been taken some years back.

"That picture was taken by *National Geographic*. One of them came up and went out with him for a week, seining. He caught a lot of fish. He was a big fisherman. My dad had five boats. The first one he had was *Jericho*. He had the *Ralph II*, *Yankee*, *Karen Jean* and *Mermaid*. The *Mermaid* was his. I took over from him. The last boat he owned was *Karen Jean*. *Karen Jean* had that Allis Chalmers in there, pretty small. Dad called it an eggbeater. He replaced it with a Cat. He sold me that engine for one dollar. I was on my way over to Excursion one day when the boat stopped. We thought we hit something, so my son went down to the engine room. He said steam was

The Greybeards

coming out of the side of the engine. I had it five or six years before that happened. Boy, sure was economical for fuel."

He just laughed when I asked him if he was as good a fisherman as his dad was. He pointed to another picture on the wall. It was the *Mermaid*, and she was loaded down to the guards with fish. Though he couldn't remember how many pounds were on board that particular trip, he commented that the boat could pack 26,000 fish. I assumed he meant pinks or humpies. At an average weight of three pounds each, that would be 78,000 pounds, a fairly hefty load in anyone's book. His best season, as he recalls, was 800,000 fish, something he is justifiably proud of.

"You know that Maxine's boy, he's got that one boat? He's always bragging about catching ... ahh ... a million pounds. How many pounds is 800,000, just humpies? Three pound average."

I quickly did the calculation in my head. "Holy smokes, Jake, that's 2,400,000 pounds!"

He started chuckling. He was understandably pleased with his prowess as a fisherman. Fortunately, once the fish were on board, they didn't have to deal with them again.

"We didn't pitch it. We pulled up alongside the tender, and they had that pump. It don't take long to pump it out, and we just go right back out."

He was referring to the vacuum pump that the tenders carry nowadays. It makes short work of emptying the fish hold. Prior to the arrival of the pumps, the fish had to be

Jake White

removed by hand one at a time, a laborious, backbreaking job that tied up the boats for hours.

I knew that the seine season was incredibly short, lasting roughly six weeks, from the end of June to the early part of August. Not much time to make a living.

"When I was fishing with my dad they used to start on June 20. Every year, June 20. It closed almost up to September. We used to fish Inian Islands. My dad really knew that area. Fish and Game closed it for experimental closure, they called it. It's still closed." He chuckled, knowing that once it's closed, the chances are it will never be open again.

I remember hearing of the fishing out at the Inian Islands. It's an incredibly turbulent area of water at the entrance to Cross Sound where the tides stack up and whirlpools form, and the currents can shove a boat or net up onto the rocks in a heartbeat. The passes act much like a nozzle on a hose, constricting the amount of water that can enter Icy Strait on the flood tide, thus causing the strong currents.

One stretch of water there is aptly named the laundry, for the up and down beating the boats and crew took. For those who knew the area and how to fish it, it could be lucrative. The Hoonah seine fleet had mastered that locale, and it was a real blow to the local economy when it was shut down.

I'd read that in the early days there were no hydraulics to help pull in the seine. The hydraulic power block wasn't invented until 1959, so I asked about it.

The Greybeards

"When you were working with your dad, what did you use to pull in the seine if there was no power block?"

"Just regular, just winch. Niggerheads. I don't know what they call them now, but we just call them niggerheads. You turn the winch on and wrap the line around. What do they call them now?" he asked, perhaps hoping to find a more politically correct term.

"I don't know." I laughed. "I've never heard any other name for them."

"That's all I knew," he said innocently.

"So you must have liked what you did, huh?"

"Uh-huh ... that's all we could do to survive. Gee, you know one time we only caught 12,000 fish for the whole season. There was no fish."

"So what did you do?" I asked.

"Nothing."

It was a typical one-word response to a direct question, and for whatever reason, I found it funny and started laughing. I found his candid answers not only refreshing but somewhat humorous. While I would have panicked and run off for the nearest town to try and find work, it wasn't that way with Jake and his generation. They lived off whatever the land and sea could provide. He laughed with me and then expanded his answer.

"There was no work anywhere. Even now, there is some around now — more than the time that I was fishing." He continued on. "When I was fishing with my dad, like when the season's over, in the early part of September, end of August, we skiff trolled. We had outboards. We fished for cohos, king salmon. There's buyers all over. Mostly Homeshore when the cohos were running. A lot of buyers there."

Though he trolled at the end of the seine season, he preferred to catch his fish in the net. No doubt it was a lot more lucrative than dragging hooks around, waiting for the fish to bite. I discovered that he also fished halibut with his father before the seine season started.

"You know, they didn't have any quota closing. Once it opened, it stayed open; you just keep catching."

"Do you remember how much you got paid for them, Jake?"

"Eight cents, 7 cents a pound, top price 15. Gee, once we went out, like when it opened? My father never came in. When we were going to sell, we go to Pelican. Set all our gear and then go. Then we come out, just start hauling. My dad never came in until it was time to switch (to seining)."

"Where did you like to set for halibut, or would you rather not tell me?"

"Out there, North Passage … around Lemesurier. Mostly fished the deep side. They stay there all year round, too."

I was hoping to find out if he had fished any of the places a little closer to home.

North Passage around Lemesurier Island isn't too far from North and South Inian Pass, and there is still a lot of current running, even on small tides, so if I have a choice I'd prefer not to fish there.

The Greybeards

"Have you ever fished here in the bay, Jake?"

"No."

"Why not?" I asked.

"Not enough fish. One day deal in the bay, you know. Wipe 'em out."

His answer was straightforward. It made no sense to waste time and resources fishing where there aren't enough fish to make it worth your while. I wish I had been able to crew with Jake. It would have been a learning experience.

I have a great deal of admiration for the early fishermen. They had knowledge and skill in abundance. Many had no radar or fathometer. They navigated by compass and landmarks and could look at the clouds and know what the weather was going to do. Nonetheless, accidents still happened. I asked Jake if he ever fished on the outside coast, around Yakobi Rock on the edge of Cross Sound and the Pacific Ocean.

"Yeah. Sometimes the fish don't come. They hit Yakobi, and they're going that way."

"How did you keep your nets off the rocks?"

"By the chart."

Just viewing a chart can be deceptive. You may think you are at a particular location on the chart where it is deep enough to set and find that you've misjudged and ran up onto the shallows. Now we have Global Positioning Systems that fairly accurately pinpoint your location.

"Did you ever rip the seine?" I wondered.

"Some guys did. You see some guys snag, you go there

and see where it's at." He started laughing. Like all fishermen, for the most part we don't wish the other fellow any trouble, but better him than you, and if you can learn from his misfortune, all the better.

At one time Hoonah had an extensive seine fleet. Jake thought maybe 25 or 30 local seiners used to anchor out front of town. There was no harbor or city float at the time. The only two docks available were the L. Kane dock, where Hoonah Cold Storage is located, and Hillmans dock, now known as Hoonah Trading. He thinks there may only be two or three Hoonah boats that still seine.

There was a lull in the conversation while I went over the notes and questions I was going to ask. His wife, Lilly, was in the living room having a conversation with her granddaughter during commercials on TV. Outside the bitter wind was whipping, and the chimes on the porch responded in a musical tone. I was beginning to think that perhaps I had exhausted the well of conversation when Jake got a second wind and surprised me with the revelation that he used to troll the *Mermaid*. I would think that a 58-foot seiner wouldn't be the most economical boat to troll out of; the fuel alone would be a major expense. I guess the advantage would be that you could stay out fishing long after the smaller boats had to run for shelter in a blow. Armed with a loran, Jake ventured out to fish the West Bank of the Fairweather Grounds. A loran used radio signals from two or more land stations to enable a boat offshore to pinpoint its position. It was a necessary piece of equipment for those wishing to fish the

The Greybeards

Fairweather Grounds, a shelf about 40 miles off the outside coast, between Cape Spencer and Yakutat.

"There's always fish there," he said. "I fish on the outer edge, 40 fathoms. Nobody comes there by us 'cause it takes so long to get there. On *Mermaid*, it does 10 knots, you know, 12 knots full bore. It all depends on how severe the weather is. I usually take off three hours after everybody leaves — I fish that longer, nobody in my way. We passed up a lot of boats. West Bank, that one trip, I made all 25-pound average for the whole fish. Only two or three whites, all the rest reds." (King salmon have predominately red meat, but a small percentage of the fish have white or very pale pink meat, which for some unknown reason brings a smaller price.)

"That's how come I stayed there. You can't move from a place like that. I tell everybody, but nobody comes out there — it's too far," he said, chuckling. "Everybody tell you they fish there, but we never saw them."

I'm always on the lookout for any information that I can use in my own fishing, so, as with the other fishermen I talked to, I asked Jake what he liked to use for bait out on the Fairweather Grounds.

"Herring. We filleted them. I use number nine hook, behind a flasher. Use hoochies."

"Any special color or you don't want to tell me?"

"Yeah, we had special ones we used."

I sat there at the table with my tongue hanging out, waiting to hear what the special hoochies were, but he didn't say, at least not at that time.

Jake White

"When I first started fishing out there, I lowered the gear and watched it. See how the bait is working. You got to watch your speed. That's one thing; you don't troll out there like inside, you know, slow. You got to go fast. I don't know if you ever heard of Clarence Moy? They're the ones that fished out there. When I was first going to start, he told me, don't let any boat pass you when you're trolling. Try to keep up with it. Inside you just barely crawl. You know, Tom, sometimes when the westerly was blowing, when we turned, gee, our lines would be way out, and just then the springs would be pounding, they would hit it, going that fast!" he exclaimed, surprised that the fish would take a bait at that speed.

"Some of the kings we throw on deck, you know they're flopping, they have needlefish. While they're flopping around, they fall out of their mouth. My son just grab it, use it for bait. Don't cut it; just tie it on the hook. They're so full, why do they keep biting?"

I shrugged my shoulders, unable to provide a suitable answer. Certainly if he didn't know, I sure wouldn't be able to shed any light on the issue. My uneducated guess would be that they were biting out of instinct.

"Used mostly Abe and Al (flashers) out there. Caught more with that than with anything else. Boy, you could see that thing down there, working, making a big circle. If you got your leader behind it just right, it acts like it's a fish. That's what I was telling you; I watch the bait behind there, watch how it's working, see how it's going. I had all different measurements (for leader length). The one that worked best we switched the whole gear to that length. I used 150-pound leader, it don't cut your hand. When we turn with the wind, that's when they start hitting, but it's hard to get them landed, it tears, you know. Sometimes the number nine hooks break. That's all I use, number nine herring hooks."

I was curious about how he managed to keep the herring fillet on the hook.

"We had wires on the eye when we put the fillet on; we wrapped it. Just salt it, so it stays on it, you know, don't lose it. Those Canadians — he told me about that fish.

"Those Canadians, when all the American boats run in because of the weather? Those Canadians stay there; we stayed there with them. You know, they're the ones that I think killed the fish off. Off the Inner Bank, we saw them. Six boats, going in a ring. We thought they were in the fish, so we went over there. They hit the fish all right but …" He held his hands a short distance apart.

"Too small?"

"Yeah! And they were taking it!" he spat out. "See, the Americans, they give you so many inches before you can take it. They were taking the small kings. They don't leave Fairweather Grounds until they're full. They take anything," he said disgustedly.

Alaska regulations prohibit the keeping of king salmon which are less than 28 inches in length. Apparently the Canadian government had a different set of regulations in place at that time, even though their boats were fishing off the shores of Alaska.

Jake White

"That one guy, I don't know if you know him, Toivo. Toivo Anderson. He was the first boat to fish Fairweather, him and another guy from Sitka. Toivo. That's all he fished, you know, was Fairweather. Fairweather and outside of Slocum Arm, that rock? He says that when that fish hits, you can load the boat up in a day or two. I never did go there with him. I don't know how come that guy really took to me. He showed me lots. If you see him, he won't tell you nothing," he said, chuckling.

As it was, the name sounded familiar. Though I didn't know the man, I had heard of how he and several other trollers had stumbled across the Fairweather Grounds and had loaded up their boats with king salmon. Of course, you would want to keep something like that a secret, but it wasn't to be. Whether they told a friend who told his friends who told even more people or whether a casual observer at the cold storage watched them unload their huge catch and someone followed them out, it's hard to say. Nonetheless, the Fairweather Grounds are no longer a secret, and if a person has the boat to take the weather and the intestinal fortitude to venture out there, there are times when the area can provide some phenomenal fishing.

Fishing out on the West Bank requires that the boat drift at night, and most captains don't post a watch. There have been a handful of stories of boats almost being run down by freighters passing by. Fog could also pose a problem.

"Gee, one time we were in the fog trolling there, didn't

even see that Coast Guard. That was when we first started trolling there. He asked, 'You seen any Russian boats? It's reported there's one around here. Let us know if you see any, and give us a direction.'"

Prior to 1977, foreign vessels, primarily Russian and Japanese, fished within 12 miles of the U.S. coast. They netted tons of salmon which were bound for rivers up and down the western U.S. shoreline. Of course, they wreaked havoc on the fisheries, not being subject to our regulations. Fortunately, Congress acted to prevent the total collapse of the species off our coast by enacting the Magnuson-Stevenson Act, which provided protection from overfishing by the foreign fleets. It dramatically cut down on the amount of salmon and bottom fish that were intercepted and gave the U.S. government more control over our fisheries.

"All the fishing I did, long lining, and you know, I see the steel boats, Christ, just about flop over. *Mermaid* just stays steady, that's how come I didn't want to get rid of it. That cannery owner down there, Brindle, Gregg Brindle, was the superintendent down there. I was here, and he calls me up to come down, he wants to talk to me. I went into the office; he told me that wood boats, it's not going to be good. You might not be able to sell it, too — that's the trouble. He said, get a steel boat, like *Donna Ann*? Same thing. He said, get hydraulic. Anything you want we'll put in there. Even trade. I turned it down 'cause I couldn't go all the places I go on the *Mermaid*."

"Why is that?" I asked.

Jake White

"Rough weather. I took my wife out to Fairweather when I was trolling. She came out, she was cooking for us. Summer's day, it was just glassy calm and easy swell. We went to bed. Right in the middle of the night the storm hit. Un-forecasted storm. Usually takes us from West Bank to Lituya Bay about three and a half to four hours. It took us nine hours. It was picking up steady, but it was in the night. During the day when we were trolling, there were a lot of logs drifting around, deadheads popping up here and there. I didn't want to run 'cause I might run into one. She kept telling me, 'Get up, let's get out.'" He started laughing. "I kept just lying down until it was daylight. We made it in, and we stayed about three or four days and went back out. We were going to sell at Lizianski-Pelican, and a storm hit us again. Boy, we sure took a beating. We got in, and they were going to unload us next day, there were so many boats in. I fell asleep and when I woke up, there's nobody in there. I opened the galley door, and I saw my wife going in the plane. She wasn't going to go through that again." He laughed. "I get a kick out of that. She just waved at me.

"It used to open April 15, I guess. I went out April 15; we only fish three days — most of the time we're in the bay (Lituya). Next time they switched it to May, but we didn't go out until middle of May, better weather."

I've never been to Lituya Bay myself, and chances are I never will, at least not on my boat. My friend Jim Moore, who fishes the *Aljac* and is an excellent fisherman, spoke of being forced into the bay because of weather. He

The Greybeards

shallowed up his gear and caught several hundred cohos right in the bay, but most people are like Jake, they just go in to anchor and wait out the weather. I asked him about entering the bay. I knew there was some kind of trick to it.

"They got lights there. You got to line them up, like when you're coming in. The bay is like this." He cupped one hand and drew an imaginary line on the table. "The lights like that, then you can turn in, only on the coming in tide. Breakers are 20 feet."

On July 9, 1958, a huge earthquake measuring 7.9 to 8.3 on the Richter scale, depending on the data you use, struck the coast. It shook loose an estimated 40 million cubic yards of dirt and glacier from a mountain at the head of Lituya Bay. When it struck the water, the force created a tsunami that reached some 500 meters high on the headlands, wiping out all the trees and sloshing around the bay, filling the area with debris. As it happened, there were three boats anchored in the bay to witness the phenomenon. Of the three that were there, the *Badger*, the *Edri* and the *Sunmore*, only the *Edri* left the bay intact. The *Badger* and the *Sunmore* were both anchored behind La Chausse Spit. The *Badger* was lifted by the wave over the top of the spit and later foundered. The crew abandoned the boat and boarded a skiff and was later picked up by another troller. The *Sunmore* got underway but was caught up in the wave and was swamped and the crew lost. I asked Jake if he has seen where the tidal wave hit.

"I took Lilly up there to see it, where the wave went up.

Jake White

Gee, almost went over the mountain. I know those people that got lost up there, too. Young, they were just married. They had a trolling boat from Juneau. They're running out, and then the waves caught them. I guess it flipped the boat — they never could find them. One guy, his anchor got stuck. He was trying to pull it up, and the wave got him and broke the chain. After the wave went by, it was good, so he just stayed there. Otherwise he said he could have ran with him, then he wouldn't have made it, either. Gee, the whole ocean was filled with trees. That boat that was lost up there was called *Sunmore*."

The sun that had been shining through the window was starting to fall behind the mountains, and I was beginning to feel like the end of the interview was in sight when he surprised me with a question. "You ever fish hoochies?"

"Yeah," I replied. "I like hoochies and spoons. I fish a lot of spoons. I like Superiors. Did you ever fish spoons or no?"

"Gee, when I was first going to start, every kind of spoon you can think of, I got it. I try it, and you know when you take it off they tarnish? I throw it overboard. I fish Canadian Wonders, gold bronze. Number five. They're regular spoon; it's not that funny look. I used it all over when I went up the bay to see if it would work. That Canadian Wonder worked real good.

"You used any of those hoochies that glow?" he asked.

I answered affirmatively and told him the colors I liked. He listened intently while I spoke of a particular day

The Greybeards

up in Port Frederick and the success I'd had, and he grunted approval when he heard what I'd caught.

"I like the ones that glow that blue, right on the bottom," he stated. "That one color on top. Lime with white belly. You know, they claim that king salmon is blind. You ever heard that? Everybody says they're blind. How come they go for certain color? See, you're dragging some, they won't hit it. Put something else on, they'll eat that."

No doubt if a fellow could figure out what the fish wanted at any particular time he'd retire wealthy. So far I've never spoken to anyone who knew, though there have been a few folks who certainly thought they did.

I asked him about fishing some of the areas that I frequent, like the northern end of Chatham Strait. He said he used to fish a skiff for kings around Hawk Inlet with some success, and apparently he seined the Admiralty Island side of the strait around Square Cove so much, and with such good fortune, that other boats referred to it as Mermaid Point. He spoke a little more about seining and mesh size and tides at various points. As I gathered the notepad I'd brought and prepared to get ready to go, he spoke again.

"Gee, you know, all the captains that's in Hoonah? They all fished with my dad."

"You mean all the seine boat captains?"

"All of them. John Hinchman, Frankie Wright, Richard Bean. They all got their own boats. A lot of the captains died off, too."

Jake White

"Yeah, that's kind of scary," I said. "That's why I'm doing this book. There is a lot of knowledge that is being lost."

Jake looked out the window and nodded. I shut off the tape recorder and zipped up the case with the notebook and spare tapes. I was grateful to have been able to hear a little bit of history at his table. Like so many other men of the sea, his memories bring a smile to his face as he thinks back to the days when the ocean lay wide before him and the promise of a bountiful harvest was on the horizon.

The Hobbit

The December wind was howling, slapping my face with a cold rain that trickled past my collar and down my back, giving me a chill that made me shiver. It was a typical winter day in Southeast Alaska.

I wished that I could hurry up and get inside to some warmth, but the rain had turned the recent snow on the dock to ice, and keeping my footing on the concrete float required that I slow down and step carefully.

I'd come down to the Hoonah harbor to visit a friend whose home for a number of years has been his boat, the *Judy Ann.*

The Hobbit

Though his name is Terry, he's affectionately known throughout the fleet as the Hobbit.

Back at the beginning of the fishing season, the *Judy Ann* was noticeably absent from the fishing grounds. Most fishermen can't wait for the season to begin, so it was odd for Terry not to be making an appearance. It doesn't take much weather for me to stay tied up to the float and wait for a better forecast. Increasingly, though, on days that I found fishable, a glance toward Terry's float would find his boat secure in the stall. Maybe it was the lack of fish or perhaps that blasted satellite antennae that had him tethered to the dock, but I had a feeling that his fishing days were coming to an end, so before he left the country, one way or another, I wanted to talk to him and try to get his story on paper.

I can't really recall how I first came to know Terry Shepard. I'd seen him around the docks and out on the fishing grounds periodically. I think I may even have given him a call on the VHF radio a time or two, though I didn't think he knew who I was. I guess it was just in his nature to speak to strangers; Lord knows he seems to attract a lot of attention, both from the folks he knows and those he doesn't. It's not uncommon for people visiting the harbor to stop at his boat and strike up a conversation with the man inside. If the person happens to be a tourist, there's typically a request for a picture or two. Terry usually obliges, though he can't understand what the attraction is.

"I guess they figure I look unusual enough that they need a picture."

The Greybeards

His small stature and wispy grey beard are part of the drawing factor. Dressed in a cerise-colored sweatshirt embroidered with hummingbirds and sporting a pair of plastic yellow slippers complete with pink ladybugs, he gives the appearance of being a lawn gnome. Occasionally, when the weather is warm, he dons a felt hat that he borrowed from a mule he once owned and steps out of his fortress to meander down to the bar. The two holes for the mule's ears are tied shut with old shoelaces, and a more appropriate cap for such a charismatic character would be hard to come by.

His boat is easy to spot — it's the only one in the harbor with a hull that is John Deere green and a top house painted chartreuse. It stands out amidst the mostly white trollers and sport boats that occupy the neighboring stalls. A lawn chair is set up on the cabin, and a plastic stork guards against feathered intruders. One look at the boat and it's readily apparent the fellow who owns this vessel isn't your run-of-the-mill fisherman, if there really is such a thing.

Much like his boat, Terry stands out on several fronts. His 5-foot, 1-inch frame is bent as he shuffles down the dock, his gnarled hand grasping a length of nylon fishing line tethered to a laundry basket, his chosen vehicle for transporting mail or groceries from his car to the boat.

"I don't like to use the carts — it's easier to use the basket," he says. "It's easier for me to control. Don't have to worry about it getting away from me when the ramp is steep."

The Hobbit

With a cane in one hand and his leash in the other, he pulls his basket of goodies behind him, jerking with each step, like a reluctant pet being forced to follow its owner.

When the weather permits and he feels up to a little exercise, he climbs aboard a three-wheeled adult-sized tricycle and slowly pedals around the town, making regular stops to talk to friends along the way.

As I approached his float, I could see that the curtains were drawn, but the blue light of a television screen lit the room where a figure sat motionless in the captain's chair. My advance toward the boat alerted a cat who stuck his head out behind the towel that served as a window treatment.

Terry didn't seem to notice the cat's alarm, and it wasn't until I stepped on the side of the boat and started to rock it that he turned in his seat and pulled back the drapes to see who was outside.

"Come in, come in," he said as he stepped down off his perch and walked over to unlock the door. "Come in by the hair of my chinny, chin, chin."

His voice is the pitch of people of small stature, and when he talks, it's readily apparent that he's without teeth. When I first met him, I was under the impression that he only had one tooth.

"No, I had three," he said. "One of the uppers and a lower one lined up so I could eat anything that I wanted. I'm a carnivore; I like meat. I would just chew it like a chipmunk. My teeth finally got so bad that I had to have them pulled. No teeth, no toothaches. I went down to

The Greybeards

Mexico twice to buy dentures, but I never left them in long enough to get used to them, so I just do without."

I stepped over the bulwarks and down onto the icy deck before entering his home. Once inside, the heat from his oil stove quickly drove the chill from my bones. I've come to do an interview with him for this story. Upon entering, I could smell the unmistakable scent of ground beef frying. "Do you want me to turn this over for you or move it off the hot spot, Terry?" I asked, aware that the meat was starting to get pretty well done.

"No," he replied, "I like it crispy."

Though he had just suffered a dislocated shoulder the day before that required a trip to the clinic, he abhorred being helped by anyone. It was all part of his fiercely independent spirit.

In the dim light I noticed an assortment of model cars and trucks lining the window ledges on both sides of the cabin. Near the front windows a cat was draped over the top of the television, while two others lay sleeping under the casement.

Terry pointed to a gray and white tabby and announced, "That's Mr. Gray Pants." He reached down to scratch it and was rewarded with a quick bite on the hand, which he shrugged off.

"Cats are independent. They own me, I don't own them," he proclaimed.

The table was piled high with an assortment of boxes, bags, clothes, groceries, a lamp and house plants, including a rather large avocado tree, whose waxy green leaves took up a large bit of the space between the table and the ceiling. The seats on either side of the table were hosting the overflow, with bulky bags of cat food and litter spilling off the cushions, and more jackets, magazines, gloves and junk mail poking out from any void in the space. A wire ran the length of the top house and hanging from it was a collection of brightly colored coho spoons and a few hoochies, tied up and ready to use next season. Space on most boats is at a premium, and this one was no different. Terry is a bit of a collector, though not of any one particular thing, it would seem. He likes placing orders and getting packages in the mail; however, where he'll put his treasures once they arrive is anyone's guess. I tried to clear off a small spot on the table and squeeze onto the bench but only succeeded in kicking a bowl of dry cat food beneath my feet and receiving a glare from the occupant on the television. I was searching for something to write on when he pushed a yellow legal tablet to me.

"Here, use this," he said. "You can keep that." It was typical of Terry to give away his possessions.

"Money doesn't mean a damn thing to me!" he said emphatically. "I spend it as quick as I get it. I don't want to die having a whole bunch of money on me that I haven't spent. That's what it's there for is to spend!"

The idea that he might need to save a little for some future emergency is foreign to him. He's lived life by the seat of his pants all his years, and it seems to suit him just fine.

Terry shuffled over to the captain's chair and took a

The Greybeards

seat, the only one available. He sat down stiffly and fumbled in his shirt pocket, finally retrieving a hearing aid that he positioned in his ear. "There. Now I can hear what's going on."

I searched for a place to lay the tablet, but there didn't seem to be a flat surface anywhere that I could set it on, so I just leaned against the cupboard, knocking over a glass and putting my elbow in the remnants of last night's dinner. Terry subscribes to the philosophy that if you don't want to do something, you shouldn't do it. I guess that's kind of the way he felt about doing the dishes.

Though I was primarily interested in knowing about his fishing career, his whole life was interesting, and he was especially proud of having been a long haul trucker so our conversation naturally drifted to the subject. He enjoyed driving truck and claimed to have logged more than a million miles accident free.

He worked for two brothers in California who had a contract with the government back during the Vietnam War, which he was strongly opposed to. In a bit of irony, he hauled parts for some kind of ordnance, I believe he said tail fins for bombs, to Ohio and frequently stopped to pick up hitchhikers, especially those whom he discovered were on their way to Canada to avoid the draft.

He entertained me with a story about stopping in a bar outside of Cleveland. Terry always loved the members of the opposite sex and had a particular fondness for black women. He knew that his prospects of running into a few ladies were good at this one particular bar, so he stopped for a drink before heading back to the West Coast.

"I was sitting at the bar just finishing my drink, and I noticed that the fellows on either side of me got up and left. I didn't think much of it. I paid for my drink and walked outside. I was almost to my truck when they jumped me. One of them got behind me and held a knife to my throat, and the other one started checking all my pockets."

"What did you do?" I asked.

"Well, I was standing on my tippy-toes, and the one guy was reaching in my pockets so I said, 'Do you need any help?'"

I started laughing. "Well, did he?"

"No. No, he reached in my front shirt pocket where I kept all my cash and took it and they left. It could have been worse. They could have killed me or taken my truck. I went down the road a ways and stopped at a truck stop and had my bosses wire me some more money, and I was on my way."

It seems that he took this incident in stride, just like any of the normal hiccups that come our way as we wander down the rocky path of life. We exchanged some more small talk for a minute or two before I managed to get the conversation turned to the subject of fishing and how it was that he ended up in Alaska.

"Well, in '74 a friend and I decided to hitchhike. I came north with just a backpack and a mandolin. Hitching is a tough business. You never knew where you might spend the night. One night you might be sleeping in

The Greybeards

a ditch and the next in a mansion. It made life interesting!" he said emphatically. "We started in Ketchikan and made our way up to Kodiak. My friend was a fiddle player. We used to play in the bars along the way for drinks. I spent many a night on a sawdust barroom floor, sawdust and peanut shells."

"That doesn't sound very comfortable," I said.

"No, I don't suppose it was," he replied. "But after a few drinks you really didn't notice it.

"In Kodiak there was a ship that ran aground. Someone towed it to the beach and turned it into a couple of bars with some rooms to rent for $12 a night. We played bluegrass downstairs. I also had a job washing dishes in the restaurant, but I only did that for a couple of days; the fiddle player said that we could get a ride to Homer on a gill-netter, so I took off my apron and threw it into the corner and left without collecting my wages. I didn't care … it wasn't that much money, anyway.

"That gill-netter was aluminum — damn, it was noisy, like being in an echo chamber. It was horrible. I knew then not to ever have an aluminum boat." Terry paused and looked wistfully out the window, stroking his beard with a wrinkled white hand, lost in thoughts of the past.

I waited while he reflected for a few seconds more and then asked, "Why is your skin so white? Is that part of having Brittle Bone Disease?"

He looked down at his hand before answering. "I don't know. I might be dead already and not know it. I might be decomposing," he said, laughing.

The Hobbit

He was born with Osteogenesis Imperfecta, Brittle Bone Disease. Deafness, small stature, a blue tint in the whites of the eyes and multiple fractures are all symptoms of people who have this genetic disease, and Terry has experienced all of them. However, fear of a fracture never kept him from searching out the adventure he seemed to thrive on. When he was living in Oregon, he suffered with a broken back after the motorcycle he was racing in the dark struck a log on a back road.

Before he was 12, Terry had broken the bones below his knees 38 times.

"I've had more broken bones than Evel Knievel. He just died, you know. Yes, sir, more than 50 broken bones; and then just last year I broke my hip in two places up at the post office on that ice. I'm still waiting to hear from my lawyer about that. I'll probably never see a cent of that money. The government will probably drag it out until I'm dead, and then they won't have to pay. Yep, yep. That's the way they are."

As we talked he fed himself a steady stream of Cheetos from a large bag near his chair. The yellow-orange crumbs drifted down onto his beard which bounced with the motion of his chewing. Watching him eat made me think of a bearded Cabbage Patch doll. I had to laugh at the spectacle, and Terry was quick to laugh with me. He likes to have fun and enjoys a good laugh, even at his own expense.

"I go through a bag of these about every two days," he said.

The Greybeards

I noticed a package of pork rinds on the table and asked if he minded if I had one.

"Go ahead! Hell, that's what they're there for. There's some M&M's somewhere on the table, too. Help yourself."

As we munched our snack, I asked, "When did you start fishing, then?"

"I was in Sitka, Alaska, and this fellow named Steve Lowrey was leaving to go back to New Zealand, back where he was from. He owned the *Misty Rose*, a little hand troller. He knew I liked the boat. Me and one other guy wanted it, so Steve said we could toss a coin for it, and if I won it he would sell the boat to me. A fellow at the bar flipped a coin, and I called it and won. He sold me the boat right there in Ernie's Bar. Back in those days, a handshake was as good as a contract. You couldn't do that now, though. He just tossed me the keys and walked away. I didn't even know how to put down the poles! He left all the gear onboard, so the next day I went out under the bridge and started fishing. I caught two kings my first time out. I thought, *This is pretty easy.* I bought the boat for $3,500 and paid it off in the first three months. That boat could catch fish!

"Years ago there was a fish-buying scow down at Kalinin Bay. They used to give a bottle of wine to whoever brought in the biggest king salmon. I won a bottle for a 64 pounder that I caught in the Shark Hole. I got another bottle for a 55-pound king that I caught on the other side of Salisbury Sound. I caught both fish with the *Misty Rose*. I had to quit at 2:00 every day because the fish hold was

The Hobbit

full. There was a 20-pound average on those kings. I had many a big fish break the gear. When they hit the line they would tip the boat. The seven years that I fished the *Misty Rose* was the most peaceful time of my life. I wish I'd hung on to that boat." He pursed his lips and looked down, lost in his memories for a few seconds, and then continued.

"The best trip I ever had was on the *Judy Ann*. I was fishing kings about 11 miles off the coast of Whale Bay on July 1st. All four lines were going. In a day and a half, we filled the slush tank all the way to the top, made $4,800. I had a deckhand named Susan fishing with me. She was from Port Alexander, fished with me for three years. She was unusual."

"What made her unusual?" I asked.

"Mainly because she was on the boat with me." He laughed.

Terry never hired male crewmembers, always female, for the obvious reason. Though he wasn't an attractive man by his own admission, he never seemed to lack members of the opposite sex willing to share the cramped space onboard. He did hire one gal who refused his advances for the entire season. Finally as she was packing her duffle bag to catch the ferry at the end of the season, he offered his beloved mandolin if she would share his bed.

"She said, 'Terry, I will *never* sleep with you!' and walked out the door, so I just went down to the bunk and laid down to take a nap. I was almost asleep when I felt a bare leg straddle me." He laughed.

The Greybeards

"So what happened?" I asked.

"I gave her my mandolin. I couldn't go back on my word."

Just because his crew was female didn't mean they were naturally domestic.

"I had one deckhand that'd come from a wealthy family. Apparently she was never taught how to cook. She used to open a can of tuna, dump it out on a slice of bread, put another slice on top and call it a sandwich. No butter, no mayo, nothing. She used to do the same thing with a can of mushroom soup — open the can and dump it into a pan on the stove, she didn't even add water."

He recounted another gal who never wanted to do the normal duties that would be required of the hired help. She only wanted to steer the boat, a job normally retained by the captain. He would come in from working the deck, pulling and cleaning the fish and ask if he could steer the boat now, and she refused to give up her spot. For whatever reason, he kept her on for the full season. He thought that she eventually got a job as captain of a yacht or some other commercial vessel.

The sun had long since set while I stood in the warm comfort of the top house and enjoyed the friendship of this exceptionally entertaining man, but before I left, I had one question I wanted to pose.

"What about your nickname. Did you come up with the Hobbit, or was that someone else?"

"No … that was some friends of mine. Back in the 70s, when I was still driving log truck in Oregon, I had some

The Hobbit

friends who liked to listen to my stories of adventure. They said I sounded just like the Hobbit, the character from the JRR Tolkien trilogy. I liked the name, so I kept it."

He started petting a cat, which had made its way onto his lap, and chuckled.

"Here it is 30 years later — where did all the time go?" He sat silently stroking the feline before going on. "Fishing was an adventure and a challenge. Sometimes I didn't know where I was going to anchor for the night until the end of the day." He paused again and then continued. "I feel lucky that I was able to fish for so long. I feel like I've caught enough fish, though. I'm going to sell my permit and buy an RV and spend my winters in the desert. The cold didn't used to bother me, but it does now that I'm getting older. I'll be 73 this coming February. Maybe I'll buy a sport rod and go sport-fishing if I want a king salmon to eat. Yep, yep, yep."

His announcement left me feeling a little melancholy, probably for my own selfish reasons. It's comforting to see familiar boats out on the drag, to have someone to talk to on the radio when the fishing is slow. Perhaps it's the idea that one day I may announce that I've caught enough fish. I don't want that day to come, but I suppose it's inevitable.

As I gathered my papers together and put on my jacket, he came down off his chair and surveyed the meat in the pan. "Yep, that looks like it might be done," he said, poking at the charred hamburger. I stepped out into the cold night air and said goodbye to my friend.

The Greybeards

"Well, you know where I live." He smiled. "Don't let your meat loaf."

I could hear him cackling to himself as I stepped off the boat and onto the icy concrete of the float. I waved to him as I started down the dock, feeling pretty lucky to have such a friend as the Hobbit.

Adam Greenwald

On any given summer day while on my way to or from the harbor, I might spot Adam Greenwald* in his backyard, maneuvering his riding lawnmower in concentric circles or tending to his garden or smokehouse. When I spot him sitting in his car at the store or post office, I always like to stop and chat for a few minutes. He possesses a sharp memory and an ability to hold my attention with stories of past fishing adventures, so I'm always pleased when our paths cross. Blessed with uncommon good sense and skill, his talents have served him well as a highliner in the commercial fishing fleet. He

The Greybeards

still goes out for the occasional king salmon for the table or smokehouse, but his commercial days are behind him, safe in the vault of his mind until an occasion to reminisce presents itself, and once again he relives the glory days of fishing.

I got to know Adam when I worked at the Thompson Fish Company in the late 70s. He frequently pulled up to the dock and unloaded what seemed like an uncommon amount of king salmon for a man fishing by himself out of a skiff.

In later years, after I bought a commercial license of my own, we would sometimes pass each other while I was on my way out to fish. By the time I got started, he was already done fishing for the day. I should have gotten a clue that the bite starts hours before I'm usually up and around. Occasionally I would manage to be on the water when he charged by me on his way in, giving me a quick tomahawk-chop-type wave. I noticed that he didn't fish with rods or gurdies but had customized his Penn downriggers to act as hand gurdies, thus getting the best of both worlds. Adam was like that — able to figure out the most effective way to make something work and come up with the greatest return for the effort expended.

He had a good teacher growing up. His father, Robert, was a self-made man and a pioneer in his own right. He emigrated from the Saar Valley in Germany back in the 19th century. He was 20 years old at the time.

"He was being drafted in the Army," Adam said. "His mother and brothers and some sisters were down at the

Adam Greenwald

railroad station, and my dad went on the train that was taking all the young guys to the induction area where they went in the service for training. It was before World War I; I think it was the French-German war. So when the train pulled out, he waved to his mother. He walked like he was going to go in the train, but he walked through and jumped off the other side and went down in the bushes and laid there in the bushes until after dark. Then he took off; he made it into Belgium. He told them he was German and he was trying to escape. They got him to a freight boat that was going to London and from London across to the United States.

"He had a cousin on the outskirts of New York, but before he got there, he was sort of all lost and couldn't understand a word of English. He said he was getting pretty hungry after a few days so he went into a restaurant. There was a guy sitting there and the waitress was talking to him, and he said, 'Uh, stew. A bowl of stew.' The waitress came back from giving the order to the cook, and she asked the old man, 'Can I help you?' He says, 'Stew.' He said, for a couple of months he ate stew every day."

"When did he come to Alaska?" I asked.

"Well, that was quite a big deal. His brother came over afterward: Otto, Otto Greenwald. My dad and Otto, they were in Chicago for a while, and then they went to Pueblo, Colorado, and worked in a steel mill for a couple of years. Anyhow, the gold rush started in California, and they hiked from Pueblo, Colorado, to San Francisco. I don't know exactly how long, but it took them five days to cross

The Greybeards

the Mohave Desert. They traveled just at night because it was too hot. They'd find a bush or something, and they had a tarp; in fact, Otto once went out of his head, and the old man had to slap the heck out of him, knock sense back into him. Anyway, they made it to San Francisco, and all the excitement was the big gold strike up in Alaska. They were mining up there, north of Marysville in California, so Otto got a job there. The old man said, 'Otto, we should go up to Alaska.'"

Apparently Otto didn't share the same desire to head north as his brother, but they agreed that Robert should go, and they would keep in touch; if he struck it rich, Otto would come up right away. With that agreement, they parted. Robert took a temporary job for the fall and winter mining in Concrete, Washington, and by spring had enough money to catch a tramp steamer to Skagway, Alaska. He befriended a Dutchman on the ship, and together they traveled up the Klondike Trail and ended up in Dawson, in the Yukon Territory. Unfortunately the riches he sought weren't to be found there, so after several years he headed south to Douglas, Alaska, and the Treadwell Mine. He worked there for a while, until a new superintendant came on the scene who insisted that the workers mine the pillars that were supporting the overhead. Robert disagreed with the practice and had it out with the superintendent and quit. A short time later the mine caved in.

During the few years that Robert and Otto had separated, each had moved around, and letters that each

Adam Greenwald

party sent were returned undelivered so each thought the other had met with an accident or some such thing and had died.

While working in Douglas, Robert met Elsie Johnstone whose mother was a full blooded Tlingit. Her father, an Englishman, owned the Bartlett Cove Packing Company, located near the mouth of Glacier Bay. In the days prior to canneries, the salmon were filleted and salted in large tierces and shipped south to make lox — a smoked salmon eaten with bagels and cream cheese.

Elsie's family had grown up in Hoonah, but the town lacked a school. Her mother wanted her to have an education, so they moved to Douglas, located across the Gastineau Channel from Juneau. Robert and Elsie met and were married there and started a family. The first three of their 14 children were born in Douglas.

With a desire to try farming, Robert purchased a 50-foot sailboat named the *Arc* and sailed to the northern shore of Icy Strait to Groundhog Bay. Unfortunately, there wasn't enough farmland or sunshine for a profitable farm at that location. However, Elsie's mother knew of an area across the straits that might fill the bill, so Robert checked out Spasski Bay. Liking what he saw, he had the area surveyed and homesteaded 143 acres.

"There were lots of canneries here," said Adam, "and most of them operated strictly on fish traps."

Fish traps were a series of logs floating on the water with nets suspended beneath them. The salmon swam into them and were unable to escape. They were operated by

103

The Greybeards

the salmon canneries, most of which were owned by companies outside of Alaska. Most Alaskans hated them, feeling they caught too many fish and kept Alaskans from having jobs in the industry. Traps were outlawed in 1959 when Alaska became a state.

"This Icy Straits cannery was one of the few that didn't have a fish trap, it was all seine boats, and there was a couple other canneries that had half and half — half fish traps and half seine boats — but the majority of them was only traps. Like P.E. Harris and New England Fish Company, Sebastian Stewart, Todd Packing Company, Bushman's, the cannery at Port Althorp, they were all traps.

"In the spring of the year they'd bring a big crew up. All the traps had to be re-hung every year, you know, and it was a lot of work. So, they'd come up and work on these fish traps, and in those days there was no such thing as refrigeration. That was before they ever invented refrigeration, so all the meat for the cannery, for the mess hall, was salt meat or canned, like canned corned beef. Dad went around with the *Arc* and met purt near all the cannery superintendents, and he wanted them to give him an offer or a promissory note that they'd purchase beef, chicken, eggs, pork, milk, butter, everything, you know. Purt near all of them were just happier than heck; they said, 'We'll buy it from you.'"

On the strength of the promissory notes, Robert purchased cattle from a fellow German-American, Charlie Switzer, who had started one of the first dairies in Juneau.

Adam Greenwald

He owned a good deal of property in Juneau, from the Old Glacier Highway to the present-day airfield. Switzer sold Robert Jerseys and Holsteins for butter and milk, as well as Black Angus for beef. His well-thought-out plan was coming together. In the sandy soil around his homestead, Robert took a team of horses and a manure scoop and dug out a large area for an icehouse.

"On weekends we'd go over there, and he'd take a team of horses and pull snow in the pit until it was completely full and he had it heaped up, and we'd tamp it with snowshoes; all the kids were tamping it, and that caused nothing but ice. And then he dug steps down in it and a hallway in and dug holes, and he'd shove a quarter of beef into the pits. Then he had a couple hundred chickens, you know. He bought a whole carton of small paintbrushes, about a half-inch wide, and he had a stainless steel wire, like trolling wire, and he hung it across the top edge of the holes on the nest, and these paintbrushes, there was a hole in the handle, and he just strung them on the wire and set them down out front of the nests. He had five gallons of India ink; the schools had ink wells in the desks, it was all you could get was either gallons or five gallons, and he had five gallons. Anyway, he dipped the brushes in it, and then he'd feed the chickens. After a few days the same chickens would come back with ink on their tails; their tails would hit the paintbrush when they went in to the nest, so he knew they were nesting or laying eggs, but the ones that didn't have no ink on their tail, they went to the chopping block."

The Greybeards

"How did he figure that out?" I asked. "I wouldn't have thought of that in a thousand years."

"Well, you know, his family ... was pretty ingenious. Otto, you see, he lost track of Otto. They both thought each other was dead, and my oldest brother, Albert, moved south 'cause he was fishing, and when it closed down here in the fall of the year, he went south and fished down at Puget Sound. Anyway, Albert bought a home down there in La Conner and wintered there, and a state trooper for the State of Washington bought a home right next to Albert. They became pretty good friends, and in the course of conversation he said he had been a trooper in California, in the Grass Valley area. Albert said, 'I had an uncle that used to live in Grass Valley, but that was years and years ago. I think he's dead now.' The trooper said, 'Do you know what his name is?' He said, 'Otto Greenwald.' The guy said, 'You know, I knew a Greenwald down there. He lived in Grass Valley, and he was pretty well off.'"

The trooper gave Albert the name of a sheriff in Grass Valley who confirmed that there was an Otto Greenwald living there. He was married and had several children. That fall, after the fishing season, Albert and some of his relatives, including his father, Robert, took off on a trip down to California. His dad had no idea where they were going or why, he just thought they were going on a sightseeing vacation. When they got to Grass Valley, Albert pulled up to Otto's home. Unfortunately his brother wasn't home at the time, and they missed each

Adam Greenwald

other several times before Robert tracked him down in an Oriental store, watching a card game going on in the rear of the store. When his brother spotted him, Robert went around the other side of the aisle in a game of cat and mouse. When they finally came face to face and Robert told his brother who he was, they embraced and cried. After 43 years of separation and uncertainty, they finally knew that the brother each had thought he had lost was alive and well. Otto took his newfound family back to his home.

"Down in his basement was a big lab," Adam continued. "He was an inventor. His first big invention, he had lots of smaller inventions, but his first big invention was, he invented the gum-wrapping machine, and he sold that to Wrigley Brothers, the patent and everything. Then he had two more big inventions after that. He's got a factory in Philadelphia, and his great-grandson is running the factory. One of them is a soft ice cream machine, and the other one is a coin operator for the Laundromats. You can go to any Laundromat — he's got an exclusive patent on them; it's Greenwald Incorporated.

"I've never been struck with the bug that makes me want a lot of material, you know. I've got a good living, and I'm happy. I wasn't too impressed with all the millions, but it's fine. The old man come up to Alaska to get rich, and Otto stayed down in California and become a millionaire," he said, laughing.

Adam mentioned he was one of three surviving World War II veterans here in Hoonah: his brother Karl, Jake

The Greybeards

White and Adam. I had the pleasure of interviewing all three of them. Adam was the chief engineer on an ocean-going tug out in the Aleutian Islands. I asked why the Army needed an ocean-going tug — I figured that would fall under the Navy or Coast Guard.

"We towed ammunition barges, supply barges, reefer barges, oil barges — the Army had quite a fleet of boats in the Aleutian Islands, belonged to the Army Transportation Corp. That's what I was in, the Army Transportation Corp. That was 1943. I was a little young to be going into the service at that time; I was 17.

"I sort of lucked out," he continued. "I was working for the Forest Service, driving truck."

When they discovered he had experience with boats and was able to steer a compass course, he was assigned to the *Forrester*, a boat owned by the Forest Service stationed in Juneau.

"They were going to send it down to Edna Bay to do some survey work down there. There was a big logging camp down there, logging airplane spruce. They built airplanes."

"Out of spruce?" I was a bit surprised.

"Yeah, before they ever built them out of aluminum, before that, was all fabric, there for quite a while. You probably heard about the biggest plane in the world…"

"The Spruce Goose?"

"Yeah, that plane was built out of all spruce. They could bend it, you know, and anyway, they had to have vertical grain spruce and old growth, fine grains so they could cut big, wide sheets out of it for airplanes."

Adam was transferred up to Cordova to go to work on another Forest Service boat, the *Chugach*. It was just him and the captain on the boat, so one of them had to do the cooking and cleaning, and the other had to run the boat. The captain offered to show him how to operate the engines, which opened the way for him to get a temporary diesel license.

The following fall he was drafted into the Army. While he was in boot camp, he was asked about his previous work experience. They discovered he was a diesel engineer on a federal boat, so he was put in the transportation corps and sent out to Adak as the chief engineer on an ocean-going tug. Another Hoonah captain, Jake White, worked with Adam on the tug as an oiler.

"I was on every island that had a base on it in the Aleutian Islands. We towed ammunition barges to Attu and to Shimya; we towed supply barges even to the Pribilofs and back and to Umnak and Sanack. When we had nothing else to do, we'd tow targets for the shore batteries. They had big floats with a high target on it, and we'd go off about two miles, three miles offshore, and they'd direct us to where they wanted us to go. There was about a 1,500-foot tow line."

"I don't think I'd like that," I said.

"No, I didn't like it," he replied. "There was a lot of times there was a big geyser right behind the boat. That was one of the worst hitches we had, was to tow targets for the shore batteries."

The Greybeards

Something that was said stirred a memory, and he rose stiffly from his chair and retrieved an album with a picture of Hoonah before the fire. It showed a long wooden boardwalk with buildings close together on both sides. The area was neat and orderly and reflected a time when pride in the community ran high.

"That was original Hoonah," he said, "back when they still had both sidewalks. That was tribe houses on this side, and the beach side was all private houses, and see here?" He pointed to a sign on one of the buildings. "See where it says Hoonah Restaurant? That was old man Mayeda. That was George Mayeda's father. He was an old Japanese, and when World War II started, they came in and picked him up, him and another Jap that had a bakery here, and they took them to a concentration camp. That happened all over the United States."

Talking to Adam was like walking back in time. I had heard of the internment camps, but didn't realize that they would play a role right here in Hoonah. At one time Hoonah was a thriving town. There were shipwrights, a huge seine fleet and multiple stores and a bakery. There was even a saw mill located where the ferry terminal is now. When I arrived in 1976, it had all disappeared. I asked Adam what happened.

"You know, they closed down Inian Islands for seining, and the seine fleet was sort of lost — that's where they made their money. Probably the biggest seine fleet, the local seine fleet, in all of Southeast Alaska was here in Hoonah. I've seen boats tied up that were purt near all the

Adam Greenwald

way over to Graveyard Island. More than 150 boats tied up there and then lots of them anchored out. There was boats from Oregon, Washington, all over Puget Sound and from all over Alaska. They fished the bay here, they fished all over. I can barely remember, but there were still a couple fish traps left in the bay, but there used to be fish traps all up in the bay here and all over.

"This cannery (Hoonah) never had a trap. Excursion Inlet had two canneries, and Port Althorp had a big salmon line cannery. Libby McNeil, Libby had several canneries. They had a big cannery at Taku Harbor. Did you ever see that book *The Silver Years*?"

He got up and retrieved his copy, and we spoke for a while about the canneries back in their heyday. We looked at pictures of thousands of cans of fish coming out of the retorts where they were cooked.

"They didn't box them until the cans were cool. Originally they were wood boxes, but they had cardboard boxes, oh, in the 30s they started coming out with cardboard boxes. Even the cans were shipped up; flats they called them. There were no ends in them, they were squashed flat, so one ship could haul a whole summer supply of cans. Then they had what they called the reform machine; they went through the reform machine and made 'em round, and they went down to the next machine and put the bottoms in 'em — the seamers. When I first can remember, the cans were soldered, and they put a lacquer inside 'em. So it was quite a process just making the cans."

The Greybeards

He put the book away and sat back down in his chair, and we started talking about trolling.

"When trolling first started here, in fact, some of the oldest trollers that was here, before they were trollers, they were gillnetters. Dundas Bay and all that was all open for gillnetting. If they could get in Glacier Bay ... but the ice was down so far in Glacier Bay that a lot of the places were cut off. When I was a kid, mostly halfway down was ice, it was all glacier, and Geike Inlet, there was two big glaciers in the head, one on the left and one on the right, and it came right down about a third of the way down into the bay, and the one on the right was called Wood Glacier, because it had petrified wood in the ice. Now Wood Glacier doesn't exist anymore. There isn't enough ice to make a cocktail. It's completely gone. The whole glacier melted away, and many of them are gone.

"When I was a kid, you couldn't run it at night, nobody run at night, especially big tides — big tides in the summer, hot weather, oh, it was impossible. You could go out here at Graveyard Island right out in front of town and pick up all the ice you wanted. Icebergs all over on the beach. When Esther first come (in 1948) there was icebergs, wasn't there?" he asked, looking over at his wife. "Yeah, it's just the last 30, 35 years they've really receded. You see, in hot weather and big tides, big tides causes the glaciers to calve, and so Glacier Bay was just solid packed with ice. On outgoing tide, it would all pour out into Icy Strait, and on incoming tide, it would just spread it all over, and at nighttime it was purt near impossible to run

Adam Greenwald

Icy Strait. From Point Adolphus to Lemesurier Island, it was just solid ice; you had to nose your way through it. You could go on outside on the smaller tides, just go around the big bergs. There wasn't too many power trollers that trolled inside. In fact, there wasn't many power trollers in them days, but there was them that was gillnetting, like Orville Rude, Skippy Rude's dad. He came up gillnetting, and Ernie Swanson was his partner. Ernie Swanson is the one that had the *Elfin* that Elfin Cove is named after; now, the *Elfin II*. He had a chunk of land; he had a store in there and an oil dock and they had a buying station there, and the *Elfin II* was hauling fish to the cold storage — Juneau mostly, until Pelican opened."

(Pelican, Alaska, started out as a cold storage facility in 1938 by Kalle Raatikainen, a fish buyer who tired of making the 80-mile roundtrip from Deer Harbor to Sitka Cold Storage in his packer, the *F/V Pelican*. By August of 1942, the Pelican Cold Storage froze its first load of salmon in the sharps freezers. The rest of the town grew up around the cold storage and adopted the motto: Closest to the fish.)

"We brought the first load of fish into Pelican on the *Nuisance III*, when they cut the ribbon on the hoist. That was old man Thompson, Mike's dad, was running the boat, Stanley Thompson."

Mike Thompson later started Thompson Fish Company, which became Hoonah Cold Storage after his death.

His brother, Stanley (Steamy) Thompson, did a stint as

The Greybeards

manager of the family store, L. Kane's, and later bought fish on the *Nuisance IV*.

"Before he had the *Nuisance III*, he had the *Nuisance II*. It was a 38-foot troller, but he didn't troll with it; he was just buying fish, and he'd run around to Pinta Cove, and there was a camp at Idaho Inlet. He'd pick up there, and another one at Soapstone he'd pick up, and he made his runs around. It depended on how much fish they were catching, but he could make it two days, maybe, and then he'd take off for Juneau for the cold storage. Then there was Henry Moy; his son, Clarence Moy, was the one who had the *Tillacum* built. Henry Moy had the *Celtic*, and it was about the size of the *Nuisance II*. Henry was buying fish, doing about the same thing as Stanley did. More power trollers was showing up, so they built these stations outside at Deer Harbor and down at Green Top and Hocktaheen and Graves Harbor.

"When I was a kid and in my teens, on the inside, there was mostly hand trollers — big fleet of hand trollers — and like Sandy Stevens, he had the boat *Sadie*, he was buying. He'd bring out a bunch from Juneau, tow their skiffs out, and there'd be 20, 30 of them, and some would want to go to Whitestone, and some would want to go to Outer Point Sophia. At Homeshore, they had a campsite there on Village Point. They all went out there and set up their camp close to a creek so they had running water, and they had overhauling lines; they put their anchor out and a buoy. They had this overhauling line like a clothesline, and there's a pulley out there and a pulley in here, and they'd just have a harness snap and a ring, snap it into it and pull it and out'd go their skiff, out to the buoy, and it didn't go dry, the tide didn't make no difference. In the morning when you got up, the boat was floating; you just pull it into the beach and unsnap it and hop aboard and go out and start rowing. One of the big places was Pinta Cove. Pinta Cove had, I'd say, between 30 and 50 tents. Actually in them days, there was just more fish I think, but there was a lot of fish at Pinta Cove."

"Did they use rods?"

"No, they never used rods. Rods was something that started in the 40s around here. Before that, they had this, it was linen, they called it cuddyhunk, and it looked purt near like braided nylon, that green braided nylon? It looked similar to that, the only thing was, if you weren't careful and you got jellyfish or slime on it and you just left it sitting in the sun, it would rot, just pull apart. But they had bluestone."

"What's bluestone?" I inquired.

"It's just a blue-colored stone, mineral actually, but it will dissolve in water, but its high toxin. In fact, you got to have a permit to get it now, but in them days, they used to wash a bucket full of it and just slosh it in their hatch, scrub their hatch out. It killed all bacteria; and the seines, all seines was made of cotton or linen. When they were out seining, for three or four days they didn't do nothing, just kept fishing, but as soon as they come in on the day off, they stood in line at the bluestone tank. They had a big floating tank, logs with a great big wooden tank that was corked, and it was probably 25x20 (feet). It had rollers on each end. The seines would go down into the bluestone and pull them out on the other side, just pull them through the bluestone. The bluestone killed all jellyfish and slime, all that there, it just washed it clean. It came in big sacks like coal. The canneries got it for the seiners. You could go buy it at the cold storage, you could buy bluestone for your fishing gear. It was common. Everybody used bluestone."

I did a little research online when I heard about bluestone and found that it is a mineral known as chalcanthite, a water soluble copper sulfate. It is found primarily in arid climates because it breaks down so quickly in the presence of moisture. It is sought after by collectors of minerals and crystals, but care has to be taken to insure that it is sealed in an airtight container to prevent the breakdown of the mineral by moisture in the air. Though it occurs naturally in the outdoor environment, it can also be produced chemically for use in pools or ponds to get rid of algae. In the past it has been used as a home remedy to cure various ailments, like canker sores in the mouth. However, it is poisonous, and prolonged exposure to it wouldn't be recommended.

"After synthetic came out, it just revolutionized fishing, but before that all they had was linen and cotton. A lot of the hand trollers, when they first started out, they had cotton, and they'd pull it in. Pretty soon they got away from the cotton; even before they had synthetic, they had piano wire, and it comes in spools, solid wire. They had spools about the size of a pie plate, it would be shaped like a tin pie plate back to back. It had a beveled groove, and they just twisted an eye (in the wire) and fastened a screw on it, and that's the way they started. They'd just wind it up, and as long as you don't kink it or anything, you could wind it on and wind it off. Fine little wire, the size of a broom straw would probably be about 80-pound test, and 120-pound test, you couldn't see much difference if you looked at it, but you could feel it. It would be a little stiffer, and they wound that on the spool. Wherever they wanted a leader, they put a swivel. They had a three-way swivel, a ring on both ends and one on the side. That's what they snapped the leader onto. Then they'd wind it up and come up to a leader; they just unsnap it off of there and pull in their leaders made out of cuddyhunk. Most of them didn't use but two or three leaders, was about all. Leads were about five pounds. If you started fishing really deep, you had a 12-pound lead. Then some of them would use the cotton line. About two or three feet out on the oar they had a leather strap and a rawhide, and then they fastened a snap in there and then let out the gear. Every so often they had an eye, and it was hooked on like a harness, and it was right on the oar, and when they rowed, their gear would go like that …" (he made the motion of a person rowing a boat) "… and the spoons would go, and by gosh, they fished pretty good!"

Apparently the motion of the oars would give the spoons they were dragging the proper action to trigger a strike. Adam said when the fish would hit, the angler would let the oar rest in the oarlocks and would unsnap the line and fight the fish. It was pretty ingenious. If the price of fuel continues to climb, I may be forced to revert back to the way of the old-timers. Who knows, I may even catch more fish that way than I do now.

I mentioned how hard it would be to try to row even a small boat at a place like Point Adolphus with all the current.

"Well, they didn't — they stayed in the back eddies. They fished like in Pinta Cove and up to Chicken Flats, back down again, but you know, they didn't have to buy no fuel. They come in and they'd have maybe, like cohos, they'd have maybe 15 or 20 and that was a pretty good day, but they had no expenses much. At the same time they were only getting maybe 20 cents a pound or 15 cents a pound. They fished the tides a lot. They knew when the right tide was that the fish should be biting — get out half an hour ahead so they would be in the right position to catch fish, you know.

"You wouldn't believe the amount of herring in them days," he continued. "At nighttime, calm, you would get out and listen, and all you could hear was a roar. As far as you could see, clear across to Pleasant Island, herring was spouting on top of the water. Then they started these herring reduction plants in Chatham Strait, and they had, oh, a dozen or more down there. Purt near every big inlet, like Washington Bay, Port Conclusion, Big Port Walters, Little Port Walters, Port Armstrong, all of them had herring reduction plants in there. Then they'd make

Adam Greenwald

fertilizer; they'd cook 'em down, and the solids would go into fertilizer, and the oil would go into fish oil. They had a big fleet of herring seiners. A small one would be about 65 feet; most of them run about 75 and 80 feet. They were sardiners, they came up from California. They fished sardines out in the ocean, and in the off season, they come up here and fished herring for the reduction plant. They fished 'em down so that some of the runs of herring just never recovered, and these ones around here, sometimes I'd say it looked a little better than it did 30 years ago, but then another year comes along and they look worse. I guess they're having a tough time recovering. They killed off thousands of tons of herring. I think that had a lot to do with the run of fish. Point Adolphus had piles of herring there, and there was always a lot of fish there.

"That was one of the more popular seining places was Point Adolphus and also Pleasant Island. There was a big seining fleet that hung out over there. That was a sockeye shore, and the ones that want sockeye they fish that shore, but a lot of times you didn't get quite as many fish, but what you got was more valuable. Homeshore, that's your sockeye shore, right to this day. Most of your big runs of sockeye that come into northern southeast, a lot of them wind up going up Lynn Canal. Chilkat and Chikoot have big sockeye runs, Berners Bay got big sockeye runs and sockeye go into Taku River. Your biggest runs of sockeyes goes running up that route."

We talked about fishing around the reefs at Sister's Island and Tenekee Inlet, both places that he is intimately

The Greybeards

familiar with. It's not uncommon for the strong tides to push a boat across a submerged reef if the captain isn't paying attention. In an attempt to catch the king salmon that congregate around the reefs, many fishermen will crowd the rock piles, sometimes losing one or more cannonballs or even an entire line complete with all the gear he's dragging. I was shocked when he announced that in all the years he fished, he had only lost one large cannonball. It was such an unusual occurrence that he distinctly remembered that it happened at Table Rock by Georges Island in Cross Sound. Apparently another troller turned in front of him, and he had to turn to avoid the boat and got caught up on the rock. Cannonballs are the lead weights used by trollers to pull their gear to the desired depth for fishing. When fishing very deep, 50 fathoms or more, or if dragging large numbers of flashers, cannonballs weighing up to 70 pounds are used. It's not uncommon to lose several cannonballs every season, either because of a weakness in the trolling wire or running across a high spot. At the current price of around $3 a pound, the loss of even one cannonball is a painful experience.

I asked Adam about being out in rough weather, and as I had suspected, he's seen his fair share of it. One of his boats, the *Tillacum*, seemed to handle it especially well. The name was derived from the Chinook Indian word meaning *my good friend*. It proved to be just that. Built in 1908 in Douglas, Alaska, from fir shipped up from down south, it was 50 feet overall in length with a 13-foot beam.

Adam Greenwald

It drew 6 feet, 3 inches, and combined with rolling chocks, it was able to fish in weather that kept most of the rest of the fleet tied up. According to Adam, the boat is still fishing and is home ported in Wrangell.

While the *Tillicum* proved to be a good friend, his first boat, the *Signora*, wasn't so fortunate.

"You said you had a boat sink, right? When you were fishing outside, you had a fuel problem?"

"That wasn't outside, that was inside," he replied. "Esther was with me. That was our honeymoon," he said, chuckling. "It was by Spasski. It was getting late in the afternoon, and Frank See and Hilda, my sister, was with me, and we were going to go over to Spasski to spend a night over there at my grandmother's cabin. She had a house over there; it doesn't exist anymore. So we said, well, maybe we'll catch a fish, so I dropped the gear at Outer Point Sophia and trolled along, but there wasn't much there. I caught a halibut and, I don't know, something else, maybe it was a trout. But, anyway, it started blowing up, blowing northeast to beat heck, so I said, 'I'm going to have to pull the gear and run because it's gonna get pretty nasty.' So I pulled the gear and we took off, and boy, the boat started heaving, and the next thing you know the engine started in sputtering. Oh, God, so I turned off the beach, and my engine stopped altogether. I just jumped down in the engine room. I knew it was water, so I broke the fuel line and drained a little bit, saw the gas coming and I drained the carburetor and I hit the starter and it took a little bit and putt, putt, putt, away

The Greybeards

she went. It started in to getting dark, you know, and it conked out again." He turned to his wife and asked, "What is it, three or four times that it stopped?"

"Three times," she replied quietly.

"Three times it stopped. Well, by the time I got it drained out the last time, you heard (he made the grinding sound of a starter that was losing power) no more juice in the battery. It was too rough to try to fool around with the skiff. Frank's skiff, I was towing his skiff behind me. It was a B&B, the same model as the old wooden Reinells, pretty nice skiff, but boy, it was rough out there. So, anyway, we threw some of the stuff in the skiff, and I told Frank, 'Just run the girls into the beach.' By that time it was dark. So he took off, and I told him, 'Don't worry about me, get them to the beach,' because he was pretty loaded with the three of them in there and the pile of junk we threw in. I could see the white foam for a while, and I could hear 'em. Then pretty soon they just disappeared out of sight."

Adam was alone on the boat in the darkness; the only sound was the wind and the angry swells as they crashed ashore. Without power, the steering was useless. With the engine disabled and at the mercy of the mounting waves, the boat was dashed against the rocks and began to break up.

"Pretty soon it was on her side, and pretty soon the cabin started going and then the deck started going, and I was hanging on to the stays by the side of the boat and it was pitch dark, and pretty soon there was no more boat left to hang on to, so I took off for the reef. I got in on the beach, and Frank was supposed to come back out and try to pick me up. I was out there probably about 20 minutes or so, half an hour."

I sat there listening with my mouth agape, seeing the whole scene as it unfolded before me. "Weren't you scared?" I asked. "Your boat is all destroyed …"

"Yeah, well, the boat was gone, but I was still alive. You know, you gotta do what you can do, and so, anyway, I made it in to the beach, and then I took off hiking down the beach. Frank went in by the big flats in there. The tide was going out, and a big surf was still breaking. The girls hopped out, and he helped them pack stuff up the beach so it wouldn't get wet, and by the time he got back down, the skiff was high and dry. By himself he couldn't get a big ol' heavy thing, he couldn't get it off the beach. I could walk along the beach, and I could hear *uungh, uungh, uuunghh*. I got pretty close to him, and I said, 'Whatcha gonna do?' He jumped about this high — man, did I startle him. He said, 'I thought it was a ghost!' So, anyway, that was the biggest story, I guess. The next day we hiked down and went and hiked along the beach, and there was kindling wood for a mile along the beach. Nothing bigger than the smallest boards. It was just smashed to pieces. That was my first boat that was worth anything."

"That was the *Signora*?"

"Yeah, the original name was *Senorita*. Sig Benington had it, and he didn't like the *Senorita* name, but he had a girlfriend named Nora, and his name was Sig, so he named it after her and him, *Signora*." He laughed.

The Greybeards

It was quite the story and typical, I think, of many of the men who grew up in the bush. They learned to make the best of what life threw at them. While he was recounting his adventure, he gave no indication that it was a big deal to lose his boat while on his honeymoon and practically lose his life. I'm sure the ordeal had to have bothered him, but it didn't keep him from getting another boat and continuing on with his career as a commercial fisherman.

One of the advantages of being a fisherman in Alaska is the availability of salmon for canning, freezing or smoking. Adam has a reputation for having some of the best kippered fish around, so I asked how he came by his knowledge.

"I learned that from my grandmother; actually my mother. Both of them; they smoked, we always had a smokehouse. We had a big smokehouse over at Spasski. When we'd get in between time, things would slow down a little bit, we'd get all the king salmon we wanted because my grandfather, my grandmother's husband, Bill Douglas, was a trap watchman for PAF, the cannery up at the head of Excursion Inlet. There were two canneries there at one time. There was Excursion Inlet Packing Company and Pacific American Fisheries. Excursion Inlet had some seine boats, but PAF had all traps. He worked on a floating trap, and he'd go and check it every day before the cannery tender would come along and brail the fish. You could see if there was a king salmon, you could see them swimming around, and they had big dip nets. He'd dip 'em and pull them over, flop them out of the trap."

"They didn't want the king salmon?" I asked incredulously. King salmon are the largest of the Pacific salmon and are prized by both commercial and sport fishermen. Their flesh has a mild flavor that is delightful on the grill, in the oven or the smokehouse.

"They didn't want any part of them," he replied. "In the fish house they were all sorted — humpies were in this bin over here, sockeyes in this bin, silvers in this bin, dogs in this bin, chums. So they'd run through, say, the dog salmon would go through first, and they'd adjust the iron chinks, the machines — they're called that because before that they used to come from China with a shipload of Chinese, and they did all the butchering for the salmon, but then, when they invented this machine, they just called them Iron Chinks, and they still do. They adjusted all the machines so that when the dog salmon came through, they'd whack the heads and the tails off and split them open. They'd run thousands of fish through every hour. When it come to king salmon, they were all different sizes, so you could have it take them a half hour, 20 minutes to get everything adjusted and run two or three fish through, or something like that, and then you'd have to readjust, and you'd wind up losing money, so it was too costly. They said to my grandfather, 'Take 'em, do what you want, but we don't want 'em in the fish scow.' He'd find big old mild cures, we'd call them mild cures, anything more than 20 pounds, he'd dip them out, and after they got through brailing the trap, he'd come along and bring

The Greybeards

us eight, nine king salmon. Well, we'd kipper 'em and smoke 'em, and we had canned king salmon, smoked king salmon …"

He went on to explain the processes of both kippering and cold smoking. Everything matters, from the size of the fish to the size of the fire to the brine solution. It's a painstaking procedure requiring patience and common sense and a certain degree of skill, all of which Adam has in abundance.

"It's something that's been handed down for generations," he said. "I guess my grandfather, my mother's father, he was an Englishman, but he knew the fish industry, and that's what brought him here. He was the one that taught my grandmother how to kipper fish."

While I was here, I wanted to go over some of the techniques he had employed when he was fishing. I had remembered from a previous interview that Adam had talked about fishing for spring kings with a choked herring. He never used a flasher with them, just the herring themselves. He shared with me the process that he used to get the herring to have just the right action, and when it gets closer to spring, I'll have to give it a try. It might be difficult to duplicate, but if I could master it, it could make all the difference between a profitable day and just paying for the fuel.

"I'll tell ya, I drove guys nuts!" He chuckled. "Ol' Tubbs, over at Homeshore. I was all by myself, over to Village Point, down to Groundhog Bay Point and back again, and here come Charlie, and, uh, he come by me there and I had two poles going, *boom, boom, boom*, and he speeded up so he could get alongside of me. I landed six or seven big kings, and he's out there on the deck, and he says, 'What you using, Adam?' I told him, 'Herring!' He said, 'How deep are you fishing?' I told him, 'I'm fishing five.' At that time I had five leaders out 'cause I was fishing in pretty close. Oh, he was back in the cockpit, and he was running his gear up and down, up and down, and I was going back and he was coming down and he asked, 'How many you got now?' I told him, 'Well, I'm 30,' and a little while later he come by and I had more than 40. That evening I went up into Groundhog Bay and dropped the anchor, and after I got all situated, here come Charlie, and he went right up inside of me and dropped the anchor and he went and dumped his skiff off, his punt, you know, and then he came over. He was looking at my fish; I was dumping them down in the slaughterhouse. He says, 'You caught them all today, huh?' I said, 'Yeah.' I had close to 50 kings there, and then he went back in my cockpit and he was looking in my bucket. I had all my herring in there, and he says, 'Ya know, I can't figure it out. I'm choking them just exactly like you're choking. I got one fish for the day.'"

Unfortunately, I've been in Charlie's position all too often in my fishing career. It's incredibly frustrating to know the fish are there, but you're unable to duplicate the other fellow's good fortune.

Like most fishermen, one memory sparks another, and before you know it, your mind is ablaze with days gone by

The Greybeards

and the recollection of the good times doing something you loved, and so it was with Adam. He turned to his wife of 61 years and said, "Hey, Ma, you remember when you went up with me to Glacier Bay?" She nodded and smiled.

"I made three trips there, and that was the most fish, king salmon, I ever caught in my life in any short period. I was fishing Icy Point outside, and it was blowing nasty westerly. It was only a couple of boats fishing there about as big as me, you know, seine boat size or something like that, and I kept snapping my tagline, big seas running, and it did it a couple times over two or three days. It was a beautiful sunny day; it was blowing westerly like crazy, and the tide was about three hours in, about half incoming tide, and I thought, heck, I'm gonna run on in and dump my fish off and put big, heavy taglines on and come right back out, because it was good fishing. It was rough, but, anyway, I came in through North Pass and had fair tide sailing in, and when I come by Point Carrolus, I look over and see, man, puffing and puffing, and I thought, what the heck, lots of whales. It was glassy calm in Glacier Bay there, so I turned and run right up to Willoughby Island just about high tide. I went on back to the cockpit and swung around, and I was trolling the same gear that I was fishing at Icy Point, lot of spoons and stuff, mostly spoons. I never choked much out there 'cause they bite pretty good on just about … if you have good spoons, they bite like heck. In the old days, you could get the aluminum spoon buckets. Once you got 'em (spoons) polished, they were good for 10, 12, 15 days. Then they come out with stainless steel swivels and then they get black, but you can put the iron rings right on the spoon and it helps it some. But if you put aluminum plates in the bucket, it can be a plastic bucket, and put iron rings on the hook, they'll last quite a while. There's a solution you can mix, too, and put in. Don't put stainless steel hooks on; use blued hooks. Stainless hooks are the ones that make your spoons black. When they first came out with them stainless hooks, I knew several guys who had guys they didn't like, and they'd walk down the float there and take a stainless hook and throw it in his spoon bucket, and the guy come down in the morning to go fishing and go to put the gear in and it's all black." He chuckled. "Man, that's a nasty trick."

He never finished telling me about that trip, but he mentioned another memorable one.

"One year in particular, Schoonover and I, we did a lot of running together. We had two or three days at Homeshore there, pulling fish like crazy and fishing to dark, you know, and then it dropped off. Usually after that you can get the tail end of it at Rocky Island; if not, above Hawk Inlet or Lizard Head and sometimes at the Kittens-Funter Bay. Someplace along there you'll find them, you know. They're moving that way, as long as you know the route they're going. We didn't do nothing. We went over there — couldn't catch anything."

They went on up Lynn Canal and fished False Point Retreat, Cordwood, Shelter Island and across to Saint James Bay, William Henry Bay and Solomon Island. After three days with little success, Kenny Schoonover snagged

The Greybeards

bottom and broke a tagline. That night on the anchor, Kenny decided to go back out to the ocean and start over. Adam chose to dump in the gear and try again by Cordwood Creek on the Admiralty Island shoreline.

"I got my first line in, and I was putting my second line in the water. I looked up and my first pole was going *boom, boom, boom, boom,* so I just kept putting in the gear until I got all four lines in the water; by that time, I had three poles going, and so I started pulling fish. About an hour later, I see Kenny coming down the far side. He got down close to St. James Bay there, and I run into the wheelhouse and gave him a call on the CB. I said, 'You pick me up, Kenny?' He said, 'Yeah, I can see ya.' I said, 'Well, you better come on.' He came and he dumped the gear in, and by gosh, we stayed there about a week, and then it just dropped off, but we had close to 400 kings apiece. Where were they from the time they disappeared from Homeshore — did they go down deep? You know, just above Rocky Island, if you draw a line from Rocky Island to the Kittens and about a third of the way over, you're in the deepest water of any inside water in the whole of North America. You're about 421 fathoms. (A fathom is six feet.) You look at your chart sometimes, but most of that country is 350 fathoms to 400 — it's deep. That whole Chatham Strait is deep, but that particular spot, that's the deepest. Maybe they're down there feeding on shrimp and stuff, but that's unusual.

"Fishing them spawn kings, you fish shallow, that's the only time you want to fish right up on the surface. I drag

Adam Greenwald

maybe seven leaders, but a lot of times the bottom two leaders, or three leaders if you get a king salmon on it, wasn't a spawner, it was a feeder. It's just nature's way; all salmon, when you go out in the ocean and catch them, dog salmon, humpy, sockeye, no matter what it is, you can catch them up shallow, if the feed is up, but you can go like out to the Fairweather Grounds or you can go off of Cape Cross, drag the 50 fathom edge. They're down about 50 fathoms down over the edge, and out there you find a lot of them, but as soon as they head for fresh water, or the closer they get to the rivers, that air sack up in their back when you clean them gets bigger and tougher. A lot of times when you open them up and pull the entrails out of 'em — great big air sack; you throw it overboard, and it will be floating on the water. All salmon, dog salmon, humpies, their air sack all gets bigger, because fresh water isn't as buoyant as salt water. So that's nature's way to stay up shallow and up the rivers in the fresh water. So your spawners get close to the surface. The closer to the river, the closer to the surface. That's the kind of stuff you got to be thinking like a fish."

"I never thought of that," I replied. "I'm not a very practical guy."

"I had a lot of experience from old-timers that fished 30, 40 years before; you know, I was buying fish. I was a 12-year-old kid when I started out, out there with Stanley Thompson, and I knew every fisherman out there, and I picked their brain. There was certain ones that came in every day just loaded with fish, and there was others that

The Greybeards

came in mediocre, and then there was some that had a real tough time; it was hard to make a living. The ones that was highliners, I worked on them and found out what their gear was, how fast they go, how deep, and I was just a kid so they didn't care, they could tell me anything, but you know, you catalogue that stuff."

"When you were talking to the highliners, what one thing stood out — what was it they did that made them highliners universally, or was it a number of things?"

"Well, it's a number of things. It was just that they thought fish. A lot of times they'd be fishing certain places, and all of a sudden, they'd just wander off. You'd wonder, 'Now, why are they taking off, they're still catching fish,' but they'd disappear, and you don't know where in the heck they went to, and the next thing you know fishing is dead. He knew it was going to go dead, the tide's going to change or something."

So much of fishing is knowing when to be at a certain place, at different stages of the tide. Nonetheless, there are no guarantees that the fish will be where you think they should be. I know that luck or chance play a part in the lives of fishermen, and occasionally we all have our great days — days that we rehearse again and again with friends on a long winter night or perhaps in our minds when the bite is off and we're wondering why we're working so hard for so little return.

For most of the successful fisherman, though, luck plays a miniscule part. They're observant and can piece together the circumstances; they read the water and know

Adam Greenwald

the tides and put the years of their experience to work for them.

Before I left, I wanted to ask Adam a question that I have wondered about for years.

Along the eastern end of Homeshore is a small bay that seemed to be inappropriately named. In my 33 years here, I have never seen a groundhog, so I wanted to satisfy my curiosity, and I was pretty sure Adam knew the answer.

"Why do they call it Groundhog Bay? There aren't any groundhogs there, are there?"

"It used to be, years ago, there used to be a lot of groundhogs."

"What happened to them all?"

"I don't know … they just disappeared. I think wolves moved in and killed them off. Even in Gustavus, there used to be groundhogs all over there. Yeah, there was groundhogs over there — there really was, and now there isn't any that I know of. They just disappeared back in the 30s. Before the wolves, there was too much ice, and it cut that area off up into Canada there and all the glaciers clean across, you know. They all melted away, so you take from Haines and Klukwan there and farther north you got some big glaciers clean up to Dry Bay."

As the afternoon wore on, I learned about how to determine where the unmarked entrance to Dry Bay exists, and the movement of glaciers and glacial rebound — where the land was starting to rise after the glaciers have receded. I was leaving with a general idea of when to

The Greybeards

start fishing for spring kings, where to go on a certain tide to fish for cohos at Homeshore and how to fix a herring so it runs just so to attract a king salmon. I learned a number of practical things that will be useful to me while fishing, but I also got a glimpse of this very talented man who has lived an incredibly interesting and, I'm sure, satisfying life. I left profoundly grateful for his time and for his generosity in sharing his wisdom and stories with me.

*Adam Greenwald is Karl Greenewald's brother, despite the difference in the spelling of their last names. Their names are spelled differently because of a snafu in the military that couldn't be corrected easily.

Floyd Peterson

It was with a certain degree of fear and trepidation that I contacted Floyd Peterson. Not because of anything he had done; I guess I was just a little uncomfortable talking to a guy who had attained a bit of celebrity status in the realm of commercial fishing. Though there are several exceptional fishermen in Hoonah, Floyd has been kind of like the gold standard that some folks judge their fishing by. I've known him casually for more than 30 years, but we've never really sat down and talked much. However, when I asked him for an interview, he readily agreed to speak with me.

The Greybeards

When I first entered his home, I spotted a wood and steel comb-like artifact, maybe 14 or 15 feet long, hanging in the hallway. He saw me gazing at it and explained its function. "That's a herring rake," he said. "The old-timers used to keep them aboard, and in the morning they'd run the rake through a school of herring, and they'd get caught on the spikes. Then they'd have fresh bait for the day."

It was the first time in all the years I'd been in Alaska that I'd ever heard of a herring rake. I'd just arrived, and already I was learning something new. Seeing my interest in the rake, Floyd left the room and returned a minute later with another contraption I'd never seen.

"I found this up near Burnt Point one year when I was out hunting. It's a hand troller's seat." It appeared to be hand carved from wood and was somewhat round and hollow in the middle with twine criss-crossing the center. The front of the seat was shaped to accompany the thighs of the owner, and though it was darkened from age and a bit antique in appearance, it was a thing of beauty in its own right. I had no idea that such an article even existed. I just assumed the old-timers sat on a plank stretched across the center of the boat.

I followed Floyd into his dining room and sat at the table. His house is built high up on a hill overlooking Port Frederick, and from his perch he has a bird's eye view of the boat traffic to and from the harbor. On this particular day the bay looked calm, and the water reflected the dim golden winter sun as it tried to break through the grey-white clouds. It was the kind of day that held a promise of

Floyd Peterson

spring, and I was a little surprised that Floyd wasn't out fishing. I asked him about it.

"Oh, the tides are haywire for winter fishing. I just like to fish a couple, two or three days on the break over."

"The break over?"

"After the peak — the big tides."

It seemed like I had heard that somewhere before, and I was hoping to get some understanding about it. "Why is that? Why don't they bite on the rise?"

"I don't know," he answered. "Sometimes they do, but this winter, and most winters, they don't. They bite on the break over for two or three days. So you got to be out there Johnny-on-the-spot and fish on those days. With the price of fuel you don't want to be running around burning fuel looking for more. I burn 25 gallons an hour, at three bucks a gallon. It costs me $75 to run down to Eagle Point and back, so you gotta produce when you're spending that kind of money."

The boat he has now, a high-speed aluminum catamaran named the *Silver Spoon*, has twin 250-horsepower outboards on the stern. While it takes a good bit of fuel to get where he's going, he can get there in a hurry, and if the weather comes up, he can return home quickly. It's equipped with rods and downriggers, and unlike the trollers he's owned in the past, this one is made to go in the shallows where the winter kings seem to congregate. Back when he owned the *Caroline*, a beautiful wooden tug that had been converted to a troller, he used to tow a skiff around to access the winter fish more easily.

The Greybeards

"Down around Sitka and different places, you fish deep in the winter, but around here they've always been up shallow. You do far better to run just rods and reels using a light weight in the shallows."

"Well, that kind of puts me out of the running, then," I said.

"Oh, I used to get fish with the *Caroline* and the *MarChele* dragging up in the shallows with the heavy gear, but you lose quite a few 'cause you're catching them so shallow, and they're fighting hard."

I posed the same question to Floyd that I had asked Windy: Why he caught so many fish?

"Well, I've been doing this for 50 years. See, I lost my leg when I was 17, back in 1960. We were having a beach party down there between the tunnel and the cannery, having a few beers. Drinking homebrew, I think. At that time the town was dry. Somebody had a harebrained idea to take turns jumping over this beach fire; we were roasting weenies and marshmallows and having a hell of a good time. Anyway, guys were jumping over the fire, and of course, I'm going to go a little further than the rest of them, so I ran across the road and over the bank and over the fire, and I come down on my damn knee on a rock and crushed it. Of course, this was late at night, so the next day they sent me to Juneau; at that time there wasn't any bone specialist in Juneau, and I was in pretty bad shape. Crushing the knee cut off the circulation to the lower part of my leg. They sent me to Sitka from Juneau. Two days later, Dr. Moore, Phillip Moore — he was the only bone specialist around at that time — said gangrene had set in, and they wacked her off."

"That had to be devastating to a 17-year-old kid."

"Yeah, but I think back on it, it was no big deal. A lot better than losing an arm; you know, it slowed me down, otherwise I might be dead. I was pretty wild." He laughed.

"So you were fishing then?"

"No, well, I always fished, you know. My dad ran the crab cannery when I was a little kid, so I'd fish off the dock for halibut, herring and everything that came in after the crab gurry. Those herring would get as big as Dolly Varden trout. I used to go down there and catch them and sell them to the fishermen for a nickel apiece. We would catch big halibut off the dock; never landed any of them, but we'd sure get them on. But anyway, after I lost my leg, I lost so much time in school — I was a sophomore in high school — it was almost impossible to catch up. I didn't like school, anyway, so I said to hell with it, I'm going to go to a trade school. I went to Tacoma Vocational Technical Institute and took a course in boat building where I built my first boat. It was completed in 1962. Here, I'll show you a picture of it."

He went into the other room and returned with an album and flipped through the pages until he came to a photo of a beautiful 18-foot plywood cabin cruiser with sharp lines.

"My dad helped me with the financing. We paid $700 for the materials. It had a 40-horse Evinrude with a four-horse kicker. Seven hundred bucks for the outboard motors and $700 for the materials, so $1,400 tied up in it."

"How did you get it up here?"

"I barged it up on the old *Klehowa*, the freight boat that used to come in here."

I well remembered the *Klehowa*. They were famous for damaging or outright destroying the freight they were packing to the various villages up and down the Panhandle. However, they were the cheapest way to ship goods from the lower 48 to Alaska, so you had to take your chances and hope for the best.

"They didn't drop it, huh?" (As had happened to another unhappy boat owner.)

"Well, what they did was run a forklift right under the guard. It didn't do much damage — I patched it up. It was a ply-board boat. I touched it up, you couldn't even see it.

"I bought the *Gadget* in '64. It was a 26 footer. It was a combination troller ... course back in those days you could do whatever you damned well please, power troll or sport fish or whatever. I did a combination; I had electric gurdies, and I also fished rods and reels off of it. Then in 1969 I bought the *Caroline*, a 42-foot troller."

Commissioned in 1942 for the war effort, the *Caroline* was originally used by the Army. Sometime after the war, Alf Skaflestad took possession of it and used it in his logging operation, towing logs. In 1966 she changed hands again. Jim Tinker, a shipwright at Icy Strait Cannery, bought it and pulled it up onto the ways at the cannery where he spent several years rebuilding it into a troller.

"I went down to Seattle and bought it January of '69.

Floyd Peterson

At that time a guy by the name of Norman Vanderpool owned the *Coronation*. Back in those days some of the guys would come up here early to fish, so I teamed up with Van on the *Coronation*, and we ran our boats up together in February. It took us a month. We got stuck in every damn bay along the way. One place, before you cross Queen Charlotte Sound, is called Miles Inlet. We were in there for a week, and we ran out of water. It was blowing southwest, and we were getting these squalls coming in off the ocean, and hail was stacking up; we were melting hail for water."

Floyd power trolled the *Caroline* for 21 years before selling her and having the *MarChele* built, a 43-foot Sunnfjord, which he fished for another 14 years.

"I used to charter fish. I had the knowledge, so it wasn't too bad. I never got harassed for not catching fish, but it was too much work. Marge and I were doing all the work — we didn't hire anybody. We'd get up at 5 a.m., Marge would cook breakfast for our clients and we'd go out fishing. She cooked them lunch on the boat, then at the end of an eight-hour fishing day, we'd process the fish. We had a little B&B where she'd cook dinner for them. Hell, we were putting in more hours doing that than when we were out in Cross Sound trolling. But it was sure money, it was good money. We did that for about 14 years, and I said, well, that's enough of that, we'll sell the *MarChele* and retire. Marge will run the bed and breakfast, and I'll do the whale watch thing. It's a lot easier. I have a hand troll permit and still do a little winter

The Greybeards

king fishing. In the summer, I take the tourists out whale watching."

For a number of years Floyd has successfully taken clients to view the humpback whales that populate the area during the spring and summer months. Much like the fish he's so successfully pursued, Floyd has an intimate knowledge of the whales and where to find them during different times of the year. I assumed that he spent all his time at Point Adolphus, a popular gathering place for humpbacks in Icy Strait, but he said there are just as many to be found locally in the spring, before and shortly after the herring spawn. For many of the tourists he takes out, his tour is the highlight of their trip. As part of the whale watching package, Floyd has a hydrophone he can lower to hear them as they sing.

"It's a sure thing," he says of the tour. "It's not always a sure thing that they're talking so that you can hear them with the hydrophone, but you're gonna see them doing something, breaching or whatever. In six years there was only one time that we didn't see whales. One of my engines broke down so I could only go eight knots, so I took the people down to Spasski, where we saw a bunch of whales the previous day, but they weren't there. The people were pretty disappointed; in fact, they even got on cruisecritic.com and complained, but by that time, I was pretty well established, so I had a lot of backup. I tell them that they have a 99.9 percent chance that they'll see whales, so that's almost a guarantee, but I don't guarantee them their money back if we don't see one. If they're that way about it, they can stay home; we have enough inquiries that we can replace them. I don't give a damn one way or another. It helps to be retired, too." He chuckled. "But I like to go out, it keeps me busy."

"So you would rather do that than go out and sport fish kings or fish for cohos?"

"Well … yeah, I would. In the summer I kind of miss the ocean fishing for king salmon. One of the reasons I did retire was because they put restrictions on our king salmon fishing. We had to shake the big fish most of the season — keep the cohos. It's very frustrating. That's one of the reasons I got into charter fishing 'cause you could still do it 365 days a year with no restrictions, really. It comes to the point you don't want to do that anymore, either. Its fun when the fish are around, but whale watching is kind of a blessing; it's really easy, and people are always happy."

Though his father was a commercial fisherman in his younger years, Floyd says most of what he knows he learned on his own.

"I was very inquisitive; my uncles were fishermen. Charlie Metz lived in Idaho Inlet, Bill Metz lived in Mud Bay and there was an old-timer, Charles Johnson, who I listened to. They knew the colors to use, but the gear was too heavy, so I refined a lot of it using their colors. None of them were rod and reel guys, I just picked that up on my own mostly. There were a few old-timers around, Frankie Wright, Johnny Hinchman and a few others, that knew quite a bit about hand trolling with rods and reels.

The Greybeards

Frankie had the *Mary Joanne*, and we'd hook up a bunch of skiffs on the back of the *Mary Joanne* and put a few on deck and take off to Idaho Inlet, Tenakee, Freshwater Bay and down as far as Kelp Bay, Hood Bay and Hawk Inlet. We fished them all with rods and reels in the wintertime."

It didn't sound like much fun to me. I have a hard time staying warm in the winter when I'm outside, and I know that sitting in an open skiff with snow and frigid winds blowing would be more like torture.

"It's been a good racket," he said, sighing. "Trolling is like any other job, if you don't really enjoy it, it's no use. You gotta have the incentive to get up early in the morning, get the gear in the water; you might not catch anything right away, but if you enjoy it you're gonna be up in the morning and putting in a day. Keeping track of the good fishermen and how they're doing helps to stay on top of what's going on.

"I remember one time with the *Gadget*, back in the middle 60s, I got into cohos and kings; in those days, you could keep the kings at six pounds, they didn't have to be 28 inches. They were like 26 inches. Of course, in the summer you weren't getting a lot of big kings, but we'd get like 50 cohos and 50 kings a day. We used Penn 49 reels. By God, after two or three days of that your wrists would start to squeak. The lubricant in your wrists would start to dry up. But you know at 28 cents a pound for cohos and 45 cents a pound for kings, it took 100 fish just to make $300. Seems like gas cost about the price of king salmon, about 45 cents a gallon, maybe less, I don't really

Floyd Peterson

remember. It was insignificant then. I never really thought about fuel. A lot of guys did: 'Oh, we can't go out there, fuel's too high.' Well, hey, you got to spend money to make money, you know."

"So did you fish just about every day then in the summer?" I asked.

"Well, I was making a living at it, you know; there's one year I never missed a day."

"So it wasn't like in the wintertime where you just fished certain tides, then?"

"You fished the small tides at certain places and bigger tides at other places where the tides didn't have too much effect on the gear, if you knew what you were doing. Yeah, tides mean a lot. Even in the summer. In the winter the kings aren't really feeding, they're kind of laying dormant in these little cubby holes. In the winter, on these short days, I like to stay close to home. I like to go out and fish three or four hours and come back home. You can hit these spots, work the tide, catch two or three fish and go back the next day and not catch any. You gotta give it a rest for a few days."

He paused and leaned back in his chair. "I don't know, I just always enjoyed it. I don't have any problem getting up in the morning and going out in the dark. I've had guys come ask me, 'Can we follow you out?' or 'Can you show us some anchorages on the chart?' and this and that. I say, 'Well, it took me 50 years to learn, and I'm not going to give it away.' Like I say, I might catch three or four fish in one spot, and if I have competition there, that cuts my

The Greybeards

production in half. I admire a guy and respect him if he just follows me and does whatever, but don't come and ask me for free advice. I'll volunteer advice. I was paid 10 grand one time to show a lady how to fish — she still calls me, she appreciates it so much. When I taught her I said, 'You follow my advice and do exactly what I tell you and you'll do alright, but if you stray and become concerned about what all these other guys that aren't producing are doing, you aren't going to do worth a hoot.' She said, 'I'll follow you to the T.' That was an easy 10 grand. That was the year I was having the *MarChele* built in Tacoma. I met her in Seattle, and we bought gear and I showed her how to tie knots. She was happy as a clam at high tide. She moved up to Homer. She was charter fishing the Homer Spit for a few years, then she moved up to Seward, and she's still charter fishing to this day."

Lord knows I wish I had the money to pay Floyd to teach me how to fish. I'm sure it would be a wise investment. However, just knowing how to fish and where to fish isn't always enough. I don't doubt that I could increase my catch considerably if I stayed on the outer coasts, but the weather scares me, so I spend more time running to avoid it than I do fishing. I asked Floyd if the weather bothered him at all.

"Well, with my bum leg there were times when putting in a long day, I'd have problems with my leg. There were times when I had to take it off and fish with one leg. I'd put in a half a day with and a half a day without. If it got too rough, I couldn't handle it, but I was never scared. I

Floyd Peterson

had good stabilizers, good gear. These boats can handle more than a man can. If you've got good equipment and are familiar with the hull of the boat and everything, there's nothing to be scared of."

Of course, fishing where the fish are and being able to stay on them is the secret to success. I asked Floyd about his best day out fishing.

"Well, with rods in the spring for kings, it was 51. They were about a 17-pound average. Cohos, off of Yakobi Rock with the *Caroline*, must have been the mid-80s, we had 375 cohos for 12 hours. Well, we had more than 400 fish as we'd gotten a few kings, dogs and sockeye. I pulled, Marge cleaned. We started at 5 a.m. and sold at 5 p.m. We sold to Buddy and Sandy Howard. At that time, they were running the *Dolphin*. We had 1,200 for six days. We averaged 200 cohos a day. There's guys who do a lot better now, but most of them have deckhands. You know, this was getting later when I was getting a little older. I wasn't putting in the 16-hour days; we cut 'er off at 12 hours. We were the first ones out in the morning and the first ones in." He started laughing. "They called us the marshmallow fleet. There was me, Bruce Smith and Doug Ogilvy … Doug was pretty tough, and so was Phil Emerson. Yeah, they were tough fishermen. In the summer when the cohos were running, we used to knock off early; with kings you could put in a longer day 'cause you're not catching as many. My philosophy was, if you didn't overdo it, you could stay out there and put in the time. We knew what we were doing, so we weren't beating our heads against the wall. There were four or five of us keeping track of each other on a secret VHF channel, so to heck with what everybody else was doing. We made a good living out there."

Floyd had told me once, many years ago, that if I just stayed out by Yakobi Island and fished, I'd do fine. I reminded him of that now.

"On the king openers we used to like Deer Harbor. Get out in the 30-fathom drag; don't get in on the 20s. All the derby type fishing we have now on opening day, July 1, everybody's fighting for position on the 20s. We never did that. We'd go out in the 30s and throw out 20 fathoms of gear. We were as busy as we wanted to be, with a mixture of cohos and kings on coho gear.

"One time on the *Caroline*, when we were just learning the coast, I learned enough to stay away from the pinnacles using landmarks. That was before we had a GPS; we had a flasher fathometer. I was going to take a nap, and I showed Marge the landmark and said, 'You turn around at such and such a place, and when we get fish on all four lines, wake me up.' Well, she got the landmark a little bit misconstrued and went past it toward Surge Bay and into a pinnacle; she hollered, 'We got all four lines going.' By the time I got out of the sack and got my pants on and into the cockpit, we had lost all four lines."

He chuckled. "The funny part of that was, we weren't catching, otherwise I wouldn't have been taking a nap, but I had enough gear left that I could re-rig on the way back inside. I rigged 15 fathoms of gear for inside fishing, and

Floyd Peterson

we went over to the Pleasant Island can. That afternoon we had 20-some kings, and the next day we had more than 50 or 60. They weren't big fish, but they were saleable, so it paid off. We did better there than we did outside. Of course, it's hardly ever that way anymore, for some reason. But we used to make a living at it back when you could fish 365 days a year. We'd anchor up at Pinta Cove for the night where Engstrom had a buying scow that Gunnar and Lassie Ohman ran. We used to go in, sell fish, have a toddy and a piece of smoked fish with them and go out and do 'er again the next day. We never thought about going outside, but when Fish and Game established quotas and shorter seasons, we were forced to go outside. Well, it worked out. We did make better money out there, but it wasn't as much fun as fishing in here."

I knew that it wouldn't be long before the herring would show up to spawn, and I was curious if he ever used fresh herring for bait, maybe save a few dollars.

"No, package bait seems to work, although there were times ... one time we went down to Kelp Bay, a bunch of us on the *Mary Joanne*, and of course, this was the first part of April. The herring spawn earlier down there than they do up here. Kelp Bay was full of herring. We didn't know what we were getting into. It was the first time I'd ever fished down there. There was an old guy from Angoon who showed us the way. Frankie Wright was running the boat, Frankie Sr. We got down there and put the herring net out that night, got a bunch of fresh herring. Some guys didn't use fresh herring, they used

The Greybeards

store-bought frozen herring. Damned if you could catch a fish on that store-bought herring, they smelled good and everything, but the kings were going for the fresh, strictly fresh, so we wised up in a hurry and caught a lot of herring, and we all switched."

"So were you filleting them or putting them on whole?"

"No, this was in the spring, using the whole herring."

"So you never used a fillet in the spring?"

"Not in the wintertime."

"Why is that?"

"Because the fish were feeding on whole herring," he said matter-of-factly. "In the summer when the fish are feeding on needlefish, capelin and the smaller stuff, then you use fillets."

"Boy, I'd sure like to know what you know," I said. "Fifty years, that's a long time."

"I sold my first fish actually when I was 13. I sold it to Art Berthol. Art used to come in here with the *Fern II*; this was before Mike (Thompson) was even buying fish. My dad had an old Reinell red cedar plank skiff, with a 10-horse Johnson on it. We'd go out and sell our fish to Art. Dad let me use the skiff, and I went down by the old cannery. I didn't know how to bait hooks. My dad wasn't much of a fisherman; he used plastic or wooden plugs. He had an old blue back plug that I put down about six fathoms on an old stiff rod. I got about a 12 pounder … I forget the exact weight. Art would come in once a week to buy fish, and it was about four or five days before he was

Floyd Peterson

coming in. There was no ice in town, so we were making ice cubes in the refrigerator. Someone said to stick seaweed in the belly, so I did that; every day I'd go out and stuff it full of ice cubes. When I cleaned it, I cut the backbone up by the head so the head was flopping around — I damn near cut the head off — but anyway, Art came in about three or four days later, and he just shook his head. It was hell to look at, but it was still edible, so he bought it. He showed me how to clean them. That was '55 or '56. That's the first king I ever sold. That was more than 50 years ago. I've never missed a summer, one way or another, since then."

"So, have you lived here all your life, Floyd?"

"Oh, yeah, my mom was half Tlingit, you know. She was born and raised here. My dad came up here in 1936 on a purse seiner, from the Port Orchard/Gig Harbor area. He purse seined but didn't make any money. During the war he spent time as a merchant mariner on a tugboat over at Excursion Inlet. There were German prisoners of war there. After the war he worked on a floating butter clam cannery here in Hoonah. Parks was the name of the guy that owned it.

"My dad told the story about how all the cats in town were dragging their back legs. They would eat the clam gurry, and shellfish poisoning must have killed just about every cat in town. The gurry would wash up on the beach where the cats had easy pickings. After that, he was foreman of the Dungeness crab cannery here. They had a couple old guys fishing: Everett Glover's dad, Glenn

The Greybeards

Glover, and of course, Duke Rothwell. Dad ran the crab cannery for 25 years. It shut down in '76."

I remember seeing Duke once when I first came to Hoonah. He had a boat named the *Adeline*. He was well known in town and apparently well liked. I read a short piece about him in a book published by the National Park Service about commercial fishing in Glacier Bay. According to the book, he routinely caught several hundred thousand pounds of Dungeness crab every year.

Floyd met his wife, Marge, while he was in Seattle getting patched up. He was getting off a boat with a bottle of beer in his hand when he tripped and slammed his hand into a piling, shattering the bottle and severing some tendons. She had come down from Bethel, a Yup'ik city in Southwestern Alaska, and was attending Metropolitan Business College. They obviously hit it off and have been married for 43 years. For many of those years, Marge has worked alongside Floyd in his business ventures.

"When we were first getting started, you know, they didn't pay very much for fish. She worked down at the store for a while; it was Coastal Glacier Seafood's then. She was secretary at the health center for several years and started fishing with me in the late 60s, when I got a bigger boat. She's always enjoyed it and is really good. She can clean a fish a minute. In one day she cleaned 700 fish. This one year we weren't doing very good coho fishing, so we decided to join the humpy fleet. I got Kim Thompson and his deckhand, Rob Browdy, and we went over to the Pass. I was steering, and Kim and Rob were pulling humpies.

She cleaned all 700 of them." He chuckled. "After that she said, 'No more. No more.' Now the humpy fleet doesn't have to clean them, they can sell them in the round."

North Inian Pass acts like a funnel between Cross Sound and Icy Strait. Large numbers of fish congregate there on the journey into their natal streams. Historically humpback salmon, or humpies, have been targeted primarily by the seine fleet. The smallest of the Pacific salmon, they are usually worth less than the larger species. That, coupled with the fact that they are spasmodic once they come aboard and their frantic gyrations spray blood on every surface, make them less desirable to the troll fleet. They are just too much work when there are large numbers of them around, unless the buyers will purchase them in the round, with the gills and guts intact.

I was complaining to Floyd how some guys could fish an area with a certain degree of success, but when I got there, I could fish the whole day without a bite.

"You're impatient," he said. "You got to have patience. And another thing, if you're not catching, we found out one summer fishing down around Point Adolphus, if you're not catching, go in, drop the hook, take a little nap or sit down on deck and have a beer or maybe a can of pop or something; just relax and take the day off, and be there at the crack of dawn the next morning."

"I always feel guilty taking time off," I said.

"Well, if you're not catching, there's nothing to feel guilty about. Those guys that have the big seasons just camp out. Just like Bob's buddy fishing Wimbledon.

The Greybeards

Those guys know what they're doing. They pound the hell out of it. They don't go wandering around in a daze, you know. Those guys make big money. I've got patience, but I don't really have that kind of patience where I can deal with the boats hour after hour, day after day. Maybe I'll get five, six day's good fishing, then I'm looking for that bum day so I can scoot home. I've always been that way.

"We're living in a good spot. It's too bad that more people don't appreciate it. Through the years, we've done a little bit of traveling, and we know how other people live. They lose their job, they're out of food. Here, even if you lose your job, you can still eat." He laughed.

Several hours after I arrived, I scooted the chair away from the table and started walking toward the door. I was feeling pretty good about the information I'd gotten from Floyd. Armed with the knowledge he'd shared with me, I left, grateful for his time and looking forward to the start of my next fishing season.

Jerry and Caroline Peterson

Not all people who fish for a living are men. There are quite a few couples in the fleet who have the chemistry to be able to spend long hours together, day in and day out, in all manner of trying conditions without one of the partners ending up in Davey Jones' locker. One of the couples for whom fishing seems to work is the Petersons. Though they haven't counted on it for their sole income, they have been fishing since before I came on the scene, and it's been an enjoyable part of their lives for a number of years.

They live on Lumbago Way, just a few houses down

The Greybeards

from Caroline's brother, Windy, and not far from where she was born 71 years ago. Presently they share their home with a small white Poodle named Brutus and a cockatiel whose moniker is Groucho.

Her Grandma Greenwald, mother of 14 and well versed in the ways of childbirth, helped to deliver Caroline at home. The only daughter and youngest child in a home full of boys, she was well watched over.

"I was not allowed down on the streets, down on the docks. We had a seine fleet — more than 200 boats each with six or eight guys — so that was a no-no. I was not allowed; girls just couldn't do that."

As she got older, her brothers, ever protective, insisted that she not drink, a standard that they didn't adhere to themselves. Nonetheless, spurred on by the youthful desire for an escape from the mundane, she braved the rough waters of Icy Strait, crossing the open water in a skiff to enjoy the live music at the Excursion Inlet Lodge.

Jerry, like many of the folks who call Alaska their home, is an immigrant to the state. He grew up in North Dakota, the baby in a family of 10 children. In the 1930s, a family friend introduced one of Jerry's siblings to Southeast Alaska. The seed was planted, and one by one his relatives relocated. Many of his family members made Juneau their new home. At 18, Jerry made the move.

"I was supposed to go in the Army when I turned 18, but I had an automobile accident. A friend of mine took me duck hunting and crashed his car, and by the time I was well enough to go into the service, the GI Bill wasn't in effect, so I came up here and joined my family. A lot of my family was here, so I just came up here to Alaska."

"His brother owned the dairy," Caroline stated.

"He owned the dairy?"

"Yeah, Mendenhall dairy," he replied.

"Whatever happened to it?"

"Well, it's a veterinarian clinic there now. That big ol' barn of his is a house, and the milk house is a vet clinic. Yeah, he had cows; he come up in the 30s and fished halibut a lot and worked for Juneau dairies when he wasn't fishing halibut. He fished a lot of these waters that weren't even charted, like Dundas Bay and so forth. He fished all the way out to the Bering Sea."

While in Juneau, Jerry struck up a friendship with one of Caroline's brothers. She happened to be coming to town, so her brother set up a blind date between the two. In 1959 they were married and eventually moved to Hoonah where Jerry worked with his in-laws in the family logging operation.

While we talked, Brutus joined me on the couch for a little scratching, and Groucho received a sharp reprimand from Caroline for his piercing loud whistles that threatened to drown out Jerry's voice on the tape.

"They mostly played," he said, chuckling, "they didn't log much. They knew how to do it and everything …"

"They all played," Caroline interjected. "Let me tell you. I mean, drinking was the thing. Drinking was the thing. We didn't have a liquor store here."

"Well, how did you get booze?"

The Greybeards

"Tommy Powers. Tommy Powers. He had a liquor store in Juneau and they made him. Everybody had his booze, you know, coming in, and it was, it was okay, but a lot of people drowned trying to run their boats over to Excursion to the bar or to Juneau."

"Hoonah didn't have a bar at the time?"

"No! They closed the liquor store because of the crime rate and everything. They closed it, they went dry. That was before my time."

Apparently in an effort to prevent the bootlegging of liquor and the subsequent loss of life by those attempting the dangerous crossings to buy it, some of the town elders decided it was time to open a liquor store again, but with hours they could control.

"I know my dad and them were all involved," she said, "because it was my dad, Frank See, Joe White, William Johnson and who's the other ones … that decided it was time to get their own liquor store. That took the pressure off of the grocery stores. Some people would drink anything, anything with alcohol … Aqua Velva, Mennen's, bean curd, mouthwash."

Having run the liquor store for some 33 years, from 1964 to 1997, Jerry had seen all aspects of human behavior. "Some of these guys would be drinking shaving lotion," he commented. "One guy comes in and he says, 'Jade East! I smell Jade East!'"

While we had a good laugh, it was nonetheless a look into the desperate state of those who had succumbed to alcohol and could no longer control their desires.

Jerry and Caroline Peterson

I finally directed the conversation around to the subject of fishing. It was a little confusing to sort out the answers with both Jerry and Caroline answering the questions at once and the bird injecting a high-pitched whistle every few seconds.

"When did you all start fishing, then?" I asked. (Groucho shrieks.) I looked at Caroline and said, "I guess you always did." I just assumed it was part of her lifestyle growing up in Hoonah.

"I always did," she said. "We did that as young kids …" (Groucho pipes up from the cage with a shrill yelp.)

"Well, I fished in Juneau with my brothers when I could," said Jerry, apparently unaware that his wife was still talking. "But then I come out here (Groucho whistles) and got in a skiff and fished."

"So you fished out of a skiff with rods?" I asked him.

"Yes," Caroline answered.

"Uh-huh," said Jerry. "I didn't have to buy a hand troll permit, I just got one, and it was transferrable." (Groucho gives a half-hearted screech; I guess he was winding down.)

"Do you know when that was?" I inquired.

Caroline: "Had to be uh …"

Jerry: "Uh, I don't know when I got it, but …"

Both at once: "Sixty-four."

"Whenever it went limited entry, whenever I got a permit," he continued. (Groucho was strangely silent for a few seconds; perhaps he was trying to sort out the conversation, too.)

The Greybeards

"Yeah, I think he started hand trolling in 64, because we moved out here ... I think in 63?" she questioned.

"Yeah, it was the next year I got a skiff and started trolling ..."

"Yeah, it was the next year," she established.

"... fishing around town here," he finished. "Still do it. My horizons haven't gotten far."

A more valid observation would be hard to come by. In the 30-some years that I have known them, I've never seen the Petersons venture too far from Port Frederick on any of their fishing excursions. Most of their angling has been done in the area from Whitestone Harbor to Point Adolphus, with occasional jaunts across Icy Strait to Homeshore during the coho season. I did spot them once down in Iyoukeen Cove in Chatham Strait, but as soon as the fishing slowed down, they were trolling their way back to Whitestone.

"These slow boats don't ... I like to go someplace in a fast boat. If I had a fast boat, I would range farther," he explained.

"When we had the *Lutefisk*, we did," she said.

"We'd travel all over," he confirmed. "When we had that Reinell, we'd go to Flynn Cove and Adolphus and Pleasant Island and Homeshore and Whitestone all in one day, but with these slow boats, you can't do that. You don't buy a lot of fuel, either. I do miss a fast boat, but I'm not going to change, so ..."

Some years back Caroline had a bout of vertigo while out fishing and is in no hurry to repeat it. When the

Jerry and Caroline Peterson

weather gets rough she is ready to head for shore. The motion of the boat could trigger another episode. Consequently they don't venture too far from home. Another reason for staying close by is Brutus.

"We have that pesky dog," said Jerry, "and I've got to row him to shore."

"He won't go to the bathroom on the boat," she said, laughing.

"First thing in the morning and last thing at night; you don't get up in the morning to go fishing, you get up in the morning, rain or storm, and row that little dog to shore. The same thing at night, when you're all tired and want to anchor up and go to sleep, you got to row that shitting devil little dog to shore," he spat out.

"We've done everything," she added. "We've done everything under the sun to get him to go to the bathroom on the boat, and his tongue will be out like this (she extended her tongue) and he won't touch water, he won't touch anything, he just sits there and looks at you. We tell him, 'Go ahead, Brutus, go potty.'"

"Yeah, the money he costs us," Jerry interposed. Meanwhile, Brutus was content to sit on the couch next to me and have his head scratched, oblivious to the trouble he's created.

When out on the water Caroline is the primary navigator, and she has a reputation of being a bit aggressive on the drag. She gives no quarter when she believes she has the right-of-way. They seem to get their fair share of the fish, I guess in part because of her in-

The Greybeards

depth knowledge of the area. After all, she's fished here all her life.

"Port Frederick was our stomping grounds," she said. "We left our mark all over."

Because of their familiarity with the bay, and the many years plying the waters of it, they had nicknames for different spots up and down within it. Like most fishermen, they didn't want to share their hot spot with others, so the label they used for the various local areas helped to keep from advertising their whereabouts. I used to listen in to conversations between the different family members in the days before cell phones, when a CB radio was the primary means of communication for boats that were in close proximity of each other. It was sometimes difficult to figure out where the various parties were. One of the names I recall hearing, which was on no nautical chart, was Tillie's Glacier. I asked about it.

"That's that slide that comes down to the beach above the waterfall," explained Jerry. "It always leaves a pile of snow there."

He was referring to the steep, almost vertical hill that rises on the right-hand side of the bay between Eight Fathom Bight and the waterfall. Trees and brush have long since been torn from the sheer wall and have been unable to reclaim a foothold on the slippery slope. To this day, the snows of winter congregate in the shaded depths and remain until well into the spring.

"We didn't have freezers (in the logging camp days), so when we had our meat, our venison and that, if it wasn't

Jerry and Caroline Peterson

canned, we had to put it someplace, so my mom discovered this area that it stayed all year, so we would take our meat and bury it in Tillie's Glacier."

"So you didn't have any trouble with bears coming and digging it up?"

"If there was a bear around it was dead," she stated matter-of-factly. "In those days, they controlled them. It's not like it is now." She leaned back on the couch and continued, spurred on by the memories of days gone by. "Mom and I would have to take the flat ... we had a big green skiff, and we'd run to Hoonah, and we'd take the laundry down. We'd bring all the laundry down and do what we had to do here and shop and what have you, then we'd go back up."

Caroline's family ran a logging camp based out of Salt Lake Bay. Located on the left-hand side of Port Frederick, about nine miles from Hoonah, it was quite an excursion to make in all kinds of weather in an open skiff.

On one excursion, Caroline and her mother figured they'd try their hands at fishing.

"We decided to drop our rods and reels. We never did fish rod and reel before, so we got it all overboard by the waterfall, and we were fishing and the line took off, and there Mom and I are ..."

"You had a plug on," Jerry interjected.

"Yeah, we had a plug on, but we didn't know how to work it. We'd tighten the drag and the pole would go under the boat, we'd loosen it, and I don't know how long we fought it. We even went to shore and tried to drag the

The Greybeards

fish in — that didn't work. We finally got back in and here comes the fish, and it had to be a long time 'cause that fish was pretty dead, but it was like a 30 pounder. Boy, I tell you, Mom went and tried with the gaff hook; she got it in, and both of us pulled it up, and we were screaming and hollering. We took off and went back to camp, and, of course, they were like, 'We don't think you guys caught that.'" She started laughing. "That was our first fish we caught by ourselves.

"Dad had all those trolling boats we used to go out and fish in. I always laughed because we had red felt hats that the guys wore, and they would all be cut, some in circles, some in triangles, but everybody had a red cap. They would take them off and go jigging halibut. They would cut chunks off their hat, and that's how they jigged halibut."

I asked about some of their more memorable fishing trips. Jerry mentioned trolling up 95 cohos one day shortly after they first started fishing with power gurdies.

"And what about the day up here, across from Grassy Island?" she asked.

"Oh, Tom remembers that king salmon opening in October," he replied.

I did remember that day. October 11 of every year is the start of the winter king salmon season. One of the favorite spots to fish that is close by and occasionally produces a few kings is up in Port Frederick on the other side of Midway Island in what is known as the Narrows. The mountains rise right up out of the bay there, and you

Jerry and Caroline Peterson

can drag 15 fathoms of gear almost up against the beach. It's not uncommon for six or eight boats to rush up there in the morning of that first day in hopes of catching a few before they're all picked off. Jerry and Caroline had spent the night anchored by Burnt Point, several miles away from the Narrows. They had seen a number of blips on their video sounder and, hoping they were fish, decided to spend the night in close proximity.

"You guys had like 30 or something, didn't you?"

"Thirty one kings. Everybody was flying by," he said. "We were at Burnt Point below Grassy Island."

The Skaflestads were always a close-knit family, and if one person found the fish they would call in the other members on the CB. It was a common sight to see four or five skiffs belonging to the various relatives all fishing a given area. Lined up one behind the other, they fanned out, and using the knowledge they all possessed and the radios to let each other know what was working, they pretty much could own the section of the drag they were on. Sometimes it would be almost impossible to cut in, and I would leave the area frustrated, knowing full well that they were catching fish and wishing I had found the fish first.

"Fagan wasn't around then, but Guben was here, and he was bear hunting, I guess, or something," said Jerry. "We tried to hail him; he was scooting around. We said, 'It's good fishing here,' but he said, 'No, I got things to do.' So we said, 'Hey, that's fine.' We were all by ourselves. We got up early the next morning, thinking we were going to get a whole bunch more. We got five or six, and that was it."

We talked a bit about how the bay hasn't produced much for the past three or four years. I've spent a fair amount of time in Port Frederick myself at different times of the year — usually when the weather is inclement out in Icy Strait or I just don't feel like venturing to the outside coast. I'm always kind of hoping that there might be a repeat of the good old days when you didn't have to venture too far.

"I think we had 70 cohos one day," she mused. "Other than that, we didn't have … and then the crab pots. Three rows deep, they hold you off of the flats where you can't go into the shallows. You know, I have no problem if they want to fish crabs, but damn it, don't do it when our king salmon season is open, 'cause that blocks us from getting in."

Jerry and Caroline are both in their 70s now, and a boat is a lot of work to keep going, so I wondered if they were going to keep fishing or if they thought they might give it up.

"I don't know; if it's a slow summer, maybe we won't fish," he said. "We'll see."

"There's a lot more bother with the tourists and charter boats."

"There is!" I agreed. Until recently Port Frederick and the immediate area around Icy Strait was pretty much fished only by the local fleet, but with the coming of the cruise ships, that all changed. Often times the charter

Jerry and Caroline Peterson

boats stop and anchor in the very areas where the trollers are trying to make a pass. It makes for some unpleasant feelings and all the more so if the operators aren't local.

"Homeshore isn't fun," Jerry complained. "It's a bother, and sometimes Eagle Point and those places I fish are loaded with charter boats, and Outer Point. Then Sisters Island and those things — if there's no fish and all this bother, maybe I just won't."

He spent another few minutes bemoaning the fact that the charter fleet had grown so large and competed in the same area that they have been fishing for so many years and complaining about the huge wakes that some of them leave as they rush clients to the fishing grounds, oblivious to rules of the road or the common respect that should prevail upon the water.

"Ya know, getting back to trolling, when the price is good, then you have a lot more boats in the areas that you fish. It's harder; besides the tourists, you got all the other boats. So, it all depends on how much crap there is. I'm not going to do it for more than a couple of years at the most. I don't feel like I'm ready to sit around and do nothing, though. If we didn't have snow removal, I wouldn't have anything to do."

We lamented the impact that aging had on our bodies.

"I can't stop my age," Caroline said, "but I don't have to get old. I don't feel old. I'd go to work tomorrow."

She started working at her uncle's store, Greenwald's, in 1953 and remained there for a number of years, eventually purchasing it. When I arrived in Hoonah in

The Greybeards

1976, See's Greenwald Store was one of the three grocery stores here in town.

Talking to Caroline is a bit like being tutored by a teacher who specializes in recent Hoonah history, with a splash of gossip thrown in.

Living in a small town, and particularly if you happen to work in one of the stores, you have your hand on the pulse of the entire village. Few secrets are kept for long. I worked at both Hoonah Seafoods and L. Kane Store, and every juicy piece of gossip passed freely from customer to clerk.

We spoke of the high cost of goods now and how freight costs have skyrocketed. Everything from fuel to groceries has to be shipped in from the outside. When I first came on the scene, a tug and barge outfit called Alaska Outport was the primary means of getting goods to town. Captain Don Gallagher, one of the more colorful characters in town, had the contract to deliver the mail on his boat, the *Forrester*. He also delivered some freight from Juneau and according to Caroline, a little contraband on the side.

"He was one of the first well-known citizens of Hoonah that got picked up for bootlegging," she said, chuckling. "Imperial ... pints of Imperial; 25 bucks a bottle."

"I could write books about growing up in Hoonah and the partying," she said. "When we got married, we lived in the parking lot of the Presbyterian church, in a little hut there."

Jerry and Caroline Peterson

"The church has a lot of real estate," Jerry added. "If you didn't know that, you should, because they were the first realtors around here. The Catholic church and the Presbyterian church had a lot of land. We managed to live in a little shack between the ANB hall and the Presbyterian church."

The Alaska Native Brotherhood hall is an imposing wood-paneled building in mid-town whose grand size is offset by the fact that to this day it is unpainted, giving it a weathered look. It shares a large parking lot with the Presbyterian church. The lot is all too often filled with cars of the locals, as well as out-of-town family members who have come for yet another funeral or memorial service. Because of its large size, it serves as host for the annual local Christmas celebration, as well as other events requiring a large seating capacity. In the days before TV, local bands played in the hall, and dances were held every weekend. Built on pilings, apparently there was sufficient space and privacy underneath the building to accommodate those folks who wanted to drink. Of course, the inevitable fights followed.

"Under the ANB hall, that was the party place. If that hall could talk. The treatment plant wasn't there and neither was the trailer for the church. We called it Wino Point," she said.

"That's what it was known as. It's not our invention," Jerry added. "If they dug out all the fill around that treatment plant, there must be four feet of glass from broken bottles under there."

The Greybeards

"He built me a fence …" she started.

"The tide come in and out by the ANB hall," he interrupted, "and underneath our house even, so I had a long piece of old seine that I made a fence out of. It was pretty high, eight or 10 feet high, that's just how long it was so I used it, long enough to go around the house and keep the drift out. Anyway, I come home from work one night, and Caroline said there's something in the back of the house, and I went and looked and there was a fellow hanging upside down by his heel in the fence. He said he tried to jump over it or something. He could still talk and stuff. I got him out."

We spoke of all the changes that have taken place — like towns all across America, I guess — but somehow Hoonah has undergone even more than most, I think. From the days when the Tlingit first sought shelter at her shores, to the influence of the earliest Presbyterian missionaries, from a sleepy fishing village to a logging community to a tourist attraction. The town has been ravaged by fire and resurrected. Buildings and people have come and gone, and lifestyles have changed down through the years.

What once was is no more and will never be again, and so I'm glad to get a glimpse into the past and some of the people who have forged a life in this ever-changing environment.

I sat on the couch scratching the dog while we gossiped some more and talked about family. It was a pleasant way to spend a few hours on a winter's day.

Jerry and Caroline Peterson

When it came time to go, I thanked them for their time and left, feeling like I had a better understanding not only of my friends, but of the place I've called home for so many years.

Karl Greenewald

When I asked Karl Greenewald, Adam's brother, if he would do an interview about fishing, he agreed to speak to me as long as it wasn't official. I wasn't sure what that meant, but for as long as I've known him, he's been a joker, so I took along my tape recorder and hoped for the best.

"So, you're writing a new book, huh? Well, if it's anything like that goddamned last book you wrote …"

"Well, it won't be near as good because it's got you in it," I said, laughing.

"I was already in one," he replied.

Karl Greenewald

He was referring to the passage in *Wilderness Blues* where I mentioned the stinging label he gave me after I lost the first three king salmon that bit my hooks, No Fish Tom. I'd never trolled before and had no idea that you needed to stun the fish before attempting to gaff them. I would see him in the parking lot at Hoonah Seafoods or up at the post office, and without fail he would address me as "No Fish." My repeated attempts to relieve myself of the title fell on deaf ears, no matter how many fish I caught afterward.

"So you're starting a new book," he repeated.

"Well, I just want to have a book before everyone is gone," I said. "Johnny (Hinchman) is gone now, and Richard Bean is gone." They were two of the many seine boat captains who made Hoonah their home.

"You think about it, Johnny is gone and Richard Bean is gone, and right now there is only three of us left that fished in Indian Islands." (He pronounced Inian Islands, Indian Islands.)

"You and who else?"

"Sam Hanlon, Jake White. Jake White and Sam Hanlon. He had the *Kathy H*. It's pretty good-sized metal, maybe it's still around, I don't know. He fished almost all his life. Eli Hanlon, I don't know if you knew him, that's his brother."

"Eli Hanlon — Windy said he had a boat building shop or something down here," I said. "I'm pretty sure he said it was Eli."

"No." Karl shook his head. "No, no, no."

The Greybeards

I was afraid I was going to have a conflict of memories from two of my interviewees, but when I went back and looked at the transcript, I realized I had messed up on the name. Eli Sharclane was who Windy had mentioned.

"Right down here they had a big boat shop." He pointed downhill to the harbor fill area.

"That belonged to Elijah Sharclane, who was Eli Sharclane's grandfather. Where Bowen is? That belonged to uh, oh, hell, uh, Lonnie Houston. He had a big boat shop. He made all the coffins, for anybody that died."

"So he used to make coffins, huh?"

"Oh, he made coffins and anything you wanted. He built boats mostly, that was his trade, building the skiffs."

"Oh, skiffs, he built skiffs? He didn't build trollers?" I had assumed that anyone with a boat building shop would build something larger than a skiff.

"Yeah, yeah. You remember the *Don't Worry*? He built that. You see how my mind goes back?"

"That's what I want to know," I replied. "You guys know stuff I never even knew about. I was thinking, crap, Karl will probably die before I ever get a chance to talk to him."

"You know, I'm 82 years old, it's time for me to go." He laughed and continued on. "Here on Lumbago Flats, all the old trollers, workers, loggers, them all lived up on Lumbago Flats. I can name every one of them. They were all white people, you know. Swan Austin, George Smith. I used to love George Smith, when I was a little kid. That's where Hanlon lived, Ernestine's place. Clarence Moy built

Karl Greenewald

that, and George Smith had a house there, and we'd go up there to visit and he'd be, 'Oh, come on in.' He used to give us sugar. He'd pour us a little cup of tea and then give us sugar so we could dip it in the tea, dunk it. We liked him. He was good to us kids. You remember them things."

For a number of years, Karl worked on a seiner. Because of the shortness of the season, I inquired about work in the offseason.

"I've never been without work," he answered proudly. "I was always proud of myself, I could find work, and I'd take any kind of job. Any kind of job is a good job. I worked as a cop there for one winter. I'd get only 75 cents an hour. I never in my life, not once, took welfare or no handouts. I just got too much pride."

He bought his first crew hand license in 1941 and fished for a few years before a three-year stint in the Army. When he got out in 1947, he crewed with his older brother, Albert, on his seine boat, the *Reliance*.

"When they built these seine boats, or any of these boats around here, did they use the spruce and stuff?"

"No, no, definitely not," he replied emphatically.

"What did they use?" I asked.

"Either cedar, yellow cedar was one that they used to build the skiffs with, and the bigger boats they had to ship in fir."

"Was there yellow cedar here at the time, or did they have to get that in from elsewhere, too?"

"Oh, no, there's a lot of yellow cedar around here. You go up the bay, we used to log in, oh, South Bight, North

The Greybeards

Bight; you go up the hill, you know, all these telephone poles for years in Juneau were all yellow cedar. We logged them by hand. We'd cut 'em, knock 'em and peel 'em. We peeled them all the way down, completely, right to the tip."

If chainsaws were around then, they weren't being used by Karl and the rest of the crew. They used a two-man bucking saw, nick-named the Swedish Whip. A falling ax with a 16-inch blade was used to undercut and keep the saw from pinching. With these primitive hand tools, the crew was able to log the hillside in a fairly efficient manner.

"We were doing exactly the same thing they're doing now, the only thing is we layed it down better, where it wouldn't break, 'cause we were logging for trap pile, and they wanted more than 100 feet; but if you break one in half, hit a stump, they're no good, so you didn't get the money out of it. We'd lay it right down in between stumps. Yellow cedar, when we stripped the bark off, just give 'em a shove and it goes just like a whip, down, right out to the water. It's slippery. You think about it. I think Ben Watson, this is in North Bight, we're up there cuttin' pile and then stripping and it was quiet 'cause we were taking the bark off, and we didn't notice, but he was trolling out there. He was trolling up in North Bight, in a skiff. They didn't have outboards then, it was all rowing. We shoved one of the logs and that log was just a whipping down the hill, and it come scootin' down to the water right in front of him. He damn near died." He

Karl Greenewald

laughed. "I don't think it would have hurt him, it had that whippy tip. The tip, why you left it like that was so that it didn't drive into a stump. It comes to a stump, it goes around it."

They did most of the logging for poles and piles in the spring when the sap was running in the trees. The bugs hadn't hatched yet, either. By June they were out of the woods and getting their seines ready for the upcoming season.

"In later years we would start halibut fishing. We were the only boat out of Hoonah that was halibut fishing for years. We fished Glacier Bay, North Inian Pass and the flats there and Point Adolphus, and the big icebergs would be coming out. We used to fish halibut with glass balls. Our buoys were glass balls. We had about 20 glass balls on each buoy, six-inch balls. The reason for that was … guess."

I assumed it was so they would float higher and be easier to spot.

"That's just the opposite of what it was; they wouldn't float better. See, soon as the tide started running, they'd sink to the bottom, the icebergs drifted over top of them. I've seen some of the new fishermen, halibut fishing, come in, and didn't know how, and used kegs, and they'd stay on top and them big icebergs used to come and just go sailing out, you'd see them out by (Cape) Spencer. That's where, on Lemesurier Island, that point there, they call it Iceberg Point? Icebergs used to pile up there. I've seen them on Point Adolphus, big, enormous icebergs, bigger

The Greybeards

than the ANB hall would be up there on the beach. I've seen, when the icebergs are really coming out, a lot of guys don't realize, they think I'm bullshitting them, when they're coming out with the tide, out of Glacier Bay, the tide is strong. The mouth of Glacier Bay is shallow; it's only 25 to 35 fathoms. The icebergs hit there and stop, but tide pressure on them would roll them, and I seen 'em, *boom, boom*, just rolling out of Glacier Bay."

Though we both fished for halibut, it was apparent that our lingo was different. Karl was remembering how it used to be, and I was presenting the modern terms for the same items. When I asked if he used stuck gear, also known as conventional gear, where the hooks and gangions are weaved directly into the ground line, or if he used snap on gear, where the hooks are snapped onto the ground line as it peels off the long line reel, he looked at me quizzically for a moment before he understood the question.

"Oh, it was all conventional," he said. "We used to ganse every hook."

"To what? What does that mean, ganse?"

He looked at me with false disgust. "You," he said, shaking his head. He went on to explain that the old halibut hooks didn't have eyes to tie the gangion to. They were J hooks that had a flat spot on the top of the shaft that widened out. The hook was wrapped with tarred line, and the line was cut at the proper length. It was hard to imagine that a hook would be made without an eye in it, but that's the way it was then. His brother, Albert, used to

Karl Greenewald

bring coils of long line to him, and he spent his winters gansing the hooks onto the line.

When he was first starting out fishing, he seined with James Grant, whose grandson, Kenny Grant, owns the seiner *Inian Queen*, a solid wooden boat with a history of bringing in impressive loads of fish.

In the days before the Inian Islands were shut off to seining, they were a popular and profitable place for the Hoonah fleet to fish. The currents in North and South Inian Passes can reach speeds of eight to 10 knots, faster than many rivers flow, and there are frequently whirlpools, kelp islands and logs that could catch in a seine and foul or tear it. There are also strong back eddies that flow in the opposite direction of the tide, up against the shoreline.

It was in these strong currents that Karl found himself one day while rowing the seine skiff. I was amazed to find out that the skiffs were just rowboats with one end of the seine attached, but I was even more flabbergasted when he mentioned he fell into North Pass.

"I'm the only guy alive who ever swam through North Inian Pass," he stated nonchalantly.

"You swam through North Inian Pass? How the hell did that happen? Where were you at?"

"In one of them skiffs, in a 19 ½-foot tide, right off the blinker there. If you're ever out there, take a look at it. It sucked that skiff right straight down."

"How come you didn't go down?"

"I did go down."

The Greybeards

"Oh, Jesus, Karl! How did you get out? Were you wearing a lifejacket?"

"No. I had a pair of boots on. When I came up and looked, the boat was just swinging. Albert was running the boat then, the *Reliance*, and every time he'd kind of swing like that," he made a sweeping motion with his arm, "he'd put her in gear and wide open and the tide would just … and the seine would wrap around him — just tore the seine to hell trying to get to me. I came up, and the tide would take me back down. I took my boots that I had on (heavy rubber hip waders) and I tore them off, just like a piece of paper. I tore them boots right down to where I could kick them off. I didn't try swimming, only when I was coming up. Soon as I headed up and got air, I'd just paddle, let the tide take me. We were going across, almost to Taylor Bay, and Art Andrews was aboard, John Lawson was also aboard the boat. I could hear guys a hollering, and I heard four whistles one time when I came up, and here was the boat, *Joanne*, and it was coming from Middle Pass and had seen what happened, boy, wide open, ya know, and every time that goddamn tide hit, it just swung the boat around, and it was having a hell of a time. Art Andrews threw a line just as hard as he could, and it landed there, and I said, 'Art, leave it there, I can make it.'

"I started swimming and I just grabbed the line, and I was just putting it over my head, and I heard the guys say, 'He's gonna make it!' I looked up and there's the *Joanne* right alongside of me and the crew on there, all with life preservers and all happy. Anyway, Art and them, they

Karl Greenewald

pulled me in and threw me on deck, and I walked into the galley and they poured me a cup of coffee, and my brother, he run into the room and he come out with a nice big bottle of Jim Beam. He took the coffee and threw most of it out, and he filled most of it up with Jim Beam and said, 'Here.' That damn stuff tasted good! I took that, and it settled me down, and I thought what the heck. They went back out, they had a lot of work to do, so I just sat in the galley, I didn't show myself. The whole bunch, there was, uh, Joe White, William Johnson, Robert Grant, every boat out there was out looking for me, and they were talking on the radio at that time to Jack Templan's wife, Doris Templan, at Hoonah Trading. Well, it was a long time before it was Hoonah Trading, but that's the only communication we had between the boats, anyplace. You want to get a message into Juneau, you had to go down there, and they'd get the wire and send it in. If I wanted to send you a message, I'd have to wire you. Like Western Union. If you got a wire that come in, they had a big loudspeaker above the store; they'd pick up the phone and say, 'Hey, Tom Botts, we got a wire for you here.' You would go up to the store to get it. We had radios on the boats, ship-to-shore and ship-to-ship."

For whatever reason, Cecelia, Karl's wife, never received the news that her husband had been rescued. She went home believing that he had drowned in North Pass. Meanwhile, the crew on the *Reliance* recovered the seine net, which was pretty well shredded by the prop while they were attempting to retrieve Karl. They pitched off the fish

The Greybeards

they had to a tender and decided to run to Hawk Inlet and get another net and a new seine skiff. They had to pass by Hoonah on the way to get the net and skiff, so they decided to drop in and spend the night. At around 2 a.m. they pulled into Hoonah, so Karl elected to go home and see his wife.

"All these boats are looking for me out there, and they're talking between each other, and they can't find me, and they all thought I drowned, so my wife's working at the store down there listening to every damn thing. When I came home at 2 a.m., we were living up on Hill Street. So I look up the hill and the lights are on, and I thought, *What the hell is going on?* My old lady better not be having a party. This is bullshit! I come walking in the door, and here, all the old ladies in town were sitting down crying. I feel bad every time I think of it," he said, laughing, "but, yeah, she did not know. She almost had a heart attack. She tried to get up, she couldn't even get up."

The incident at North Pass wasn't his only near-death experience. After he took over ownership of the *Reliance* and became a captain, he was in Hawk Inlet at the Peter Pan Seafoods dock. He was there to pick up his power skiff from the warehouse. A steamship had just unloaded its cargo of more than 2,000 pallet boards, which were still on the dock. He towed his skiff out to the dock, but because of the congestion, he couldn't maneuver with the jitney that was used to tow the skiffs around the dock, so he left it and went in to get a forklift to finish the job. His son, Karl Jr., Sonny, wanted to ride on the forklift with him,

Karl Greenewald

but he couldn't take time to watch him. When he came back with the forklift, the whole dock collapsed. He rode the forklift down into the water where it immediately sank.

As he was foundering in the water, debris from overhead was crashing down on top of him. He tried unsuccessfully to get out from under the rubble for several minutes before he finally made it to a piling and could see light above and swam for the light and surfaced. His crew hand, Hank (Tex) Kaze, saw what happened and ran down the gangplank and got into the cannery's web skiff and pulled Karl out.

"They said I was under more than five minutes. Cecilia's brother, Phillip, was standing right across from where I went over. I come out of the water and I was looking, and the first one I seen was Phillip, and I said, 'Phillip, you son of a bitch!' I said, 'Where in the hell is Sonny? I'll kill you!' And I would have. If Sonny was down there and he was standing up there doing nothing, I would have killed him. Here, Sonny was right behind me, just jumping up and down, screaming like hell. I looked up, and there he was, he was right up there on the edge of the dock. I didn't care. I went down, I got in the skiff, Hank got me in the skiff, I got aboard the boat and made some coffee — I'm good.

"In come old man Charlie Jim from Angoon. Charlie Jim. He had the *Santa Rose*. That was the name of his boat. He come in and he said, 'Karl.'

"I said, 'What, Charlie?'

The Greybeards

"'Oh, you make me so happy,' he said. 'I want to tell you something.'

"I said, 'What's that, Charlie?'

"'You never have to worry about anything.'

"'Why?'

"'You're gonna live to be an old man.'

"'How do you know that, Charlie?'

"He said, 'He don't want you.'"

"That's amazing, Karl," I commented. "I think you like it in that damn cold water." He just kind of brushed it off, as if it happened every day.

"I've had lots of … the experiences I've had. I had a box of shells, of .225, go off in my back pocket, every shell."

He proceeded to tell me about a hunting trip with his brother, Albert, Big John Tine and Kenny Schoonover. They took the *Reliance* out and borrowed Frank See's skiff to tow along so they could ferry to the beach. They were going to hunt the outside coast at Portlock Harbor. It sounded foolish to me to run clear out there when there were so many places to hunt that were so much closer, but Karl assured me that the hunting there was superior. For whatever reason, they decided to stop at Port Althorp and anchor, so Karl and Kenny separated from the other two and went around inside Cross Sound and anchored behind Table Rock. He shot a forked horn, and as he was dragging it down, he met up with Kenny in a muskeg. They looked out over the water and saw that the sky had turned black. Before they could reach the beach, the storm

Karl Greenewald

hit. The skiff was tossed violently about in the waves and was driven up onto the beach. They were able to get the outboard off the back and grab the gas can, but the next wave covered the boat and filled it with sand. They couldn't move it, so they backed up the beach and looked for wood for a fire. The wind was howling, and they were both wet and cold. While Kenny was cutting kindling wood with a knife, his hands were so cold he couldn't control them, and he ended up slicing one of his fingers, almost severing it. Karl made a bandage from the bottom of his t-shirt, and they proceeded to prepare a fire. They cut twigs for beds and got quite a large fire going while the storm raged on.

"We were laying there sleeping, and oh, man, didn't that fire feel good," he said, smiling, "but it got hot, you know, so I'd roll over to the other side. I had one of those jackets you can put the ducks in the back, that kind on, and a wool jacket, so I was nice and warm. I'd roll over to one side, and then I would roll over to the other, and I had my .225, my seal gun, a high velocity son of a gun. Anyhow, I rolled over to one side and I'm cooking my butt, and pretty soon, them damn shells went off. The whole box blew up and blew my pocket off and blew that jacket almost in two, damn near blew the fire out. Kenny was laying on the other side; he jumped up and said, 'Where is it? Where is it?' He thought a bear had come … I hardly even felt it."

"Well, why would you be sleeping with shells in your pocket? That couldn't have been very comfortable."

The Greybeards

"It wasn't comfortable, anyhow," he replied. "The stars come out and the wind was blowing, it was miserable, and we wanted to stay close to that fire. But that's what happened. If you've never had a box of shells go off in your pocket, try it. I had all but three shells go off. The three shells that didn't go off was in my gun."

The conversation turned to the changes in attitude concerning the sea lion and otter populations. When Karl was fishing, common sense still prevailed. Environmental and animal rights groups were still far in the future. He preferred fishing the Inian Island area, as did most of the Hoonah seine fleet. The Inian Islands are now home to a sea lion rookery, something that was unheard of in Karl's time. I asked him about losing fish to the sea lions out there.

"In the summer, there were no sea lions at all out there. They used to sit under the blinker at North Island. If they sat there, we knocked the hell out of them. I don't give a damn, I've shot a lot of them."

"Well, now we have sea otters inside, too," I lamented. "Out at Idaho Inlet, there are rafts of them."

"I shoot every damn one I see," he replied emphatically. "I can do it legally. I shoot every one when I get a chance, 'cause I know exactly what they do. You know, on Mary's Island out in South Lizianski, the sea urchins, them big red sea urchins, would just cover the bottom. You know, if you could just get 'em now and sell them, you'd make a mint. There ain't none of that left."

Sea otters have a voracious appetite and will wipe out

Karl Greenewald

urchins, clams, crab and abalone wherever they are allowed to congregate. With the exception of tour operators, sea otters are not favorably viewed by most of the folks who make a living off the sea and those who count on it to support a subsistence lifestyle.

As the afternoon wore on, we switched gears and talked about life in Hoonah when he was growing up. His mother ran a restaurant, as well as a store, which was all connected to their house, located downtown, where Mary's Inn is now. Apparently the restaurant/store had no name at the time, or if it did, Karl didn't remember it. I asked if the cold storage was around then.

"No, no. Union Oil was, but not the cold storage. Part of the cold storage now, was the old Kane's warehouse. That's where the mail boat used to come, and they'd unload the freight and that. The old *Estebeth* used to be the mail boat, then later, it was the *Forrester*. That was in later years. Before that, it was Eddy Bock. It used to be when he'd come around the corner, *beeeep, beep, beep*. Everybody'd say Ed-dy Bock. Eddy Bock was his name. He brought the mail and everything."

"They carried more than mail, though; they brought freight, also?"

"Oh, freight. All the freight and stuff that you ordered, stuff that you could get out of Juneau. You'd have to write in maybe a week or so ahead of time, 'cause the mail had to go in on the boat. So it'd be two or three weeks before you'd get what you wanted out of Juneau."

Though there were three stores in town at the time,

The Greybeards

certain things still needed to come from Juneau, just like now.

He continued on. "I was in the store, in there watching it, when it caught afire. The building across was a tribe house, and it was on fire. Waaay burning like heck. I was on the back end, the tide was in, and I was throwing all the canned, like canned milk, cases of it, throwing it out into the water. Fruit, anything. Anything I could grab, and throwing it out into the water. Momma had a brand-new washing machine, and I tried to save that. She had just got it. She was so happy. It was one where you start the engine you know … *chg, chg, chg*. So I went and filled it — we were one of the few houses that had water. I filled it full of water so it wouldn't burn."

It was a valiant effort, but to no avail. The washing machine went the way of most of the rest of the town in that horrible fire. Shortly after the fire, he joined the Army.

"I was in the Army two months, and I was shipped down to the lower 48. They had to ship me overseas or get rid of me."

His time in the service was memorable in an unfortunate way. While in Italy, he suffered the permanent loss of hearing in one ear when an 88mm cannon went off beside him. He also had the misfortune of getting one of his feet pinched between the track of a tank and another piece of equipment. It left him without feeling in the bottom of his foot and made balancing on the deck of his boat an extra challenge.

Karl Greenewald

We revisited his fishing career. "So tell me some more about your fishing. You owned three boats, right?"

"Yeah. But I only ran one at a time," he said, stifling a smile.

Point Wimbledon in North Inian Pass is a natural gathering place for cohos in the late summer. The tides form rips that push the fish against the shoreline. I know that the trollers frequent the area, and I wondered if it was a fishable place for the seine fleet.

"What about fishing for cohos? Did you ever go over to Point Wimbledon and fish?"

"We never fished cohos. We got a certain amount of them, but we never tried. They're not a school fish. Cohos, there will be one swimming over here, one over there, maybe make a set and get 10. Where humpies are school fish, you make a set, you get 1,000. Think about it, the school fish is dog salmon, sockeye and humpy. King salmon and coho are not school fish, they're individual. You catch them every once in awhile. Say I'd get 2,000 dog salmon and for every 1,000, I'd get maybe 30 coho."

When Karl was running the boat he had a crew of eight, including himself onboard. It took a big crew to haul the net by hand and then pitch the fish off to the tenders. Karl had four different counters in his hands to keep track of the different species that they were pitching. They were paid a different price for each species, so they needed to be accounted for. Unlike now, they were paid by the fish instead of by the pound. That struck me as odd — small fish would bring the same price as a lunker.

The Greybeards

"I can tell you a good story, you talk about the little ones like that. Adam was running the *Italio* for Bob Welsh, the cannery down here. Robert, my brother, he would run the *Reliance*. We were over to Homeshore, and the goddarn sockeye, they told us, 'It's full of sockeyes over there,' so we went over there, and right by the river, by the dock that was over there, gee, it was just loaded with sockeye, but they were all underneath the dock. What we did was we pulled a seine into the power skiff. That's when he had the *Seagrams*, not the *Reliance*, he had the *Seagrams*, and the power skiff was named *Seven-Up*. That's the truth." He chuckled. "Anyhow, we were piling the seine into the skiff, and he backed into where the dock is, and we took the power skiff and we just went all the way back and forth between the piling, and when we came out to the boat and closed her up, pursed her, we had more than 5,000 sockeye. Lake Eva. That was after the war, and the piling was still there. Fish went up Lake Eva there. So we had to get rid of them, so we went over to Adam, he was running the *Italio*, the cannery tender, and we pitched them off on the *Italio*. Every one was about that size." He held his hands about 12 inches apart. "After Adam went to the cannery to unload, Bob Welsh, he was a good friend of mine, he damn near died. He tried to get us to go two to one. He said, 'I'll even lose money on two to one.' I said, 'Tough shit!'"

"Why were those sockeyes so small?"

"Different places," he answered. "Glacier Bay, in there by Sandy Cove, in that big river there? Sockeye go up

Karl Greenewald

there, and that's the earliest sockeye of any around here. They go up in May, the first part of May. They're the first sockeye to come in, and they're just little. We used to go up, long years ago, and use a beach seine. Catch them with a beach seine and use them for halibut bait."

I had never heard of a beach seine before, so I asked how it worked.

"Oh, we had all kind of tricks. You're going to be smart as an Indian pretty soon. When I quit seining…" he continued.

"When was that?" I asked.

"Oh, probably '69."

"Why did you quit?"

"They closed Indian Islands."

"Hmm. So it wasn't worth it anymore?"

"To me it wasn't," he said solemnly.

"What did you do after that? Where you retired then?"

"No, I run the oil dock. I run the oil dock more than 10 years. I used to go down and when I seen the boats come in, that hurt. That's worse than quitting smoking. Boy, that hurt, to watch the first couple years, but I got used to it. I knew every guy on there, every boat … that made it nice. I had 400 seine boats here at one time. I was running the dock. That was Standard Oil. I used to do all the ordering and everything, and we delivered all the groceries."

"Wow, 400 seine boats. Where did everyone fish?"

"Homeshore and Point Adolphus. Mostly from Whitestone up this way and a lot of them out at Point

The Greybeards

Adolphus, out at Three Hill Island; a lot of down below boats out there. See, they were originally the ones that taught James Grant, William Johnson and Joe White how to fish Inian Islands. A few Slavonians, the old-timers."

"What were they?"

"Slavonians, slavs. Yeah, and they're the ones that taught them guys how to fish."

I asked if he remembered the best set he ever made out seining. He mentioned a set he made at Excursion Inlet one fall day. He had so many fish that he called two other boats over to help, Johnnie Hinchman on the *Yankee* and Eli Hanlon on the *Lenora Jane*. Fish were spilling out of his net into theirs. There were so many fish that all three boats were loaded down to the guards.

"We got a big price for them," he said, smiling. "I had 28,000 dogs. You know, if I could just remember names, I've got lots of memories."

I could sure relate to that. Time has a way of robbing us of things we once held precious. Nonetheless, for an 82-year-old fisherman, I thought he did pretty darn good.

"What do you do all day? Do you have anything you like to do in particular?"

"I live one day to the next. I put puzzles together. I like puzzles, and then I do some carving. Make halibut hooks and stuff. I give every one away. I've never sold a thing yet. I still bead. I do a lot of beading."

He reminisced for a while longer, and then it was time for me to go. I came away with a better understanding of the person and had a chance to journey with him into the

Karl Greenewald

past — back to the days when there was a rolling deck under his feet and a crew at his command and the hopes of a big catch played through his mind.

Mike Mills

There are only a handful of die-hard skiff fishermen left in Hoonah. Amongst the few that remain are Mike Mills. His family is originally from Excursion Inlet, a large fjord north of Hoonah, across Icy Strait. One of 14 children, he's proud of his native heritage.

His father, Gilbert, was a commercial fisherman and trapper. His mother, Katherine, worked at Excursion Inlet Packing Company for 63 years. She was also an instructor at the Hoonah City Schools, where she taught the Tlingit language and culture and composed many materials for classroom use, her most widely known being the *Tlingit*

Mike Mills

Math Book. At the tender age of 13, he started his fishing career. His father showed him how to bait a hook in a way that would entice the salmon. He would give the boys a little rap on the head to get their attention when he was trying to show them something, promising that he would only show them once. Judging by his ability as a fisherman, Mike obviously listened and learned.

"My first big salmon I caught, I went up the bay with my dad. We were fishing by Westport, we went by the little reef that sticks out there, and the rod takes off. Big fish — it dressed out at 68 pounds; my first fish." He laughed. "We turned around, made another pass in there, Dad's rod took off, he had an 89 pounder. We went around the corner to Neka Bay Point, and Ed Lindoff was there. Dad thought he was hurt 'cause he was laying on the side of his boat. We went over there, tears were coming down, and he was talking to Dad in Tlingit. He told Dad the king salmon he had on, he shot it. It was so big he shot it, and the weight of it broke his line. He said it made my dad's 89 pounder look like a little one."

Though he's fished all his life, Mike never graduated from fishing skiffs to fishing a larger troller. Perhaps because for 25 years he worked most summers at the XIP cannery, and it wasn't practical to get a bigger boat. It seems that he's done just fine using the gear he had.

"At the time, we used to fish cohos at Pleasant Island. We'd leave Excursion like 8:30 or 9 in the morning and be home by 2:30 with 90-some cohos aboard; and that's rod and reel," he said. "We used to fish Black Rock shoreline.

The Greybeards

We never made it to Black Rock, though. We always started at Noon Point; we never made it to Black Rock. We'd turn around and reload. We'd run our fish here (Hoonah) to sell."

Apparently the XIP cannery, which was just a short jaunt from Pleasant Island, wasn't buying troll caught fish at the time. They were primarily a buyer of seine caught salmon and bottom fish, like halibut and black cod.

Without a doubt, running several hundred pounds of fish, plus gear and other assorted tackle, would eat up the fuel, which at today's prices would be a real consideration. I mentioned this to Mike.

"Well, it was cheap then," he replied. "At that time, we used to buy 50 gallons for $15. Now you buy 15 gallons for $50!"

We both laughed at the new reality, though it's really not a laughing matter. At the time, Hoonah had two fuel companies, the Standard Oil dock, operated by Hoonah Seafoods, and Union Oil, which shared a dock with the Thompson Fish Company.

"They sold gas at Excursion, but you had to get it from the cannery," he explained. "They had one of those old-time gas pumps. They had to pump it up first to see how many gallons were on it and then pump it down. We had to go to the office, buy the gas, they gave us a slip, we take it down to the cannery foreman with our cans, they'd fill 'em for us and we'd be on our way. A lot of our fishing was on that side, Pleasant Island, Excursion Inlet and Homeshore, where we learned the most. We went out a

Mike Mills

few times winter fishing here. We used to go out winter fishing in a skiff."

I've never really tried to fish in the winter that I can remember. I had a hard enough time staying warm with a stove close by. I've always admired the fellows who could tough it out in an open skiff when there was snow on the ground and steam on the water. I asked Mike how he did it.

"Oh, I don't know. I was probably tougher then," he said, chuckling. "Put on two pairs of socks in your boots. Dad always said if your hands got cold, stick them in the salt water."

"Really? You put your hands in that cold water?"

"It's warmer than the air," he replied. "I carry gloves now, but I hardly use them."

He used herring that his father had caught in a gillnet. He kept them salted in a barrel, and when he wanted to go fishing, he would take some out and soak them overnight in salt water to rehydrate them. In the early spring he fished right up on the beach in the shallows. His bait was a herring with the tail removed. He didn't use flashers, just a sliding sinker and the proper spin on the bait to attract the kings.

Like many of the local natives, Mike's family supplemented their income with what nature provided. "In the summertime, they used to take us out berry picking. Grandma would make it like a picnic, so when we're done, they'd have like, marshmallows, hotdogs, Cracker Jacks, soda pops and all this stuff. We'd fill up all

The Greybeards

the containers with blueberries, salmon berries, whatever they wanted. They'd jar them up. The only berries I saw Grandma freeze were Shockberries, Grey Currants."

I've eaten Grey Currants before; they have an aromatic, almost pine-like scent. They're neither sweet nor sour, and I've never really heard how to prepare them, so I asked Mike how his grandmother utilized them.

"They'd thaw them out and sprinkle sugar and seal oil on them," he replied.

"Seal oil, really? Sugar and seal oil — that doesn't sound good to me."

He rolled his eyes and moaned, indicating that I had no idea what a culinary delight I was missing out on.

"It didn't taste fishy, Mike?"

"No."

"Do you still hunt seals?"

"Only if we need them. Eat the meat, render out the fat for oil, put the oil in jars. The people use it when they boil fish, they put it in the water, or dipping, you can use it like a dip, dried fish … dried salmon you can dip in there. Some people use it in the water when they cook up herring eggs."

During the spring the herring come in to the shallows to spawn. Though there are places locally where they still spawn, it's been years since I've seen any large numbers of spawning herring. I believe most of the herring eggs come from the area around Sitka where unbelievable numbers of herring lay their eggs on the rocks and seaweed. The spawn is so thick it can be seen from the air as a white

Mike Mills

discoloration of the water. The natives cut branches from select Hemlock trees, which in itself is an art, knowing which trees have the most desirable branches, and sink them where they believe the spawn will be best. The herring spawn on the branches, and they are then collected in skiffs or larger boats and distributed. I read that some of the branches are so heavy with eggs that they are difficult to load into the skiffs. Usually there is a seiner or two who bring back the egg-laden branches to share with the rest of the town.

Like the harvesting of herring eggs, gathering seaweed has also been an annual tradition amongst the locals. While some families harvest it from Sister's Island or elsewhere, the Mills family preferred the black seaweed from Swanson Harbor, located at the corner of Icy Strait and Lynn Canal. After it's harvested, it's dried and put in plastic bags for later use. I asked how it was consumed.

"Some people put it in their fish soups. They have fish soup with rice and mix it in there. Some put it with their salmon eggs. Most the time when Mom cooked them, she'd make up a big deal of seaweed and throw the eggs with a little bacon and onions in there, and she'd serve that to us with rice for lunches."

"So you lived a semi-subsistence lifestyle, then?"

"Pretty much," he said. "We used everything; most of the meat we got, Dad brought home. He was out pretty much every day, him and Harold Dick Sr., the two buddies. They hunted in the bay, out toward Adolphus, out toward Augusta. At that time there was lots of seals.

The Greybeards

There even used to be a bounty on them."

Though there is no longer a bounty on seals, the natives are still permitted to harvest them for food and I believe for the hides as well. Mike mentioned that his grandfather used to tan the sealskins himself, and his grandmother made moccasins and gloves with the tanned hides.

Even though seals are allowed to be harvested, one traditional food that is off limits to the local population is seagull eggs. For many years, the local Tlingit returned to their ancestral home in Glacier Bay to gather seagull eggs. In 1918 the Federal Migratory Bird Act made it illegal to gather the eggs, though I know it went on for quite some time afterward. I ate a seagull egg when I worked with some of the local gals in the late 70s. When Glacier Bay was declared a national park in 1980, all hunting, as well as the gathering of seagull eggs, was forbidden.

"Glacier Bay was a pretty big thing. Mom and me used to go up every spring, gather seagull eggs. We covered them in cold water; it killed the egg so it would last longer and wouldn't mature anymore."

"How did you cook them?" I asked.

"Boil them, fry them, whatever you want, just like a regular egg. They're bigger; the yolk is pretty much an orange color, more than a chicken egg. A little bit better flavor — I think it was better. The old-timers liked to eat them with the little birds in them." He chuckled.

I've often wondered why seals were considered edible, but not sea lions. They both eat fish, and it would seem the

Mike Mills

flavor would be similar. I posed the question to Mike.

"I don't know. Probably the fat content on the sea lions is hardly there. They always told us when we were kids that sea lions would throw rocks at people, so we stayed away from them. Later on we had them as a target, we called it the target range, there was so many of them."

In recent years with the protection of the federal government, sea lion populations are again on the uptick, so much so that great colonies of them are forming in various locations around Southeast Alaska. It's no coincidence that at the same time fish populations appear to be on the decline. I can only hope that there will be a similar upsurge in the population of killer whales that feed on fur-bearing animals like sea lions and sea otters. To the best of my knowledge, the only natural predators that sea lions have are Orcas, or killer whales.

Mike's first venture into commercial fishing was in 1961. He was fishing one winter day between the old L. Kane Store dock and Pitt Island and caught eight king salmon. He sold half the fish to Frank See for 15 cents a pound and earned enough to buy a troll license. Back then, anyone could buy a commercial license and go trolling for salmon. At the time the cost was $7.00, and anyone with a skiff could become a commercial fisherman. Now the fishing industry is regulated by the State, and there are a limited number of commercial licenses available. A power troll license normally sells in the $30,000 range and hand troll licenses go for up to $10,000. While having the license allows the permit holder

The Greybeards

to sell his catch, the permit must still be renewed annually for the calendar year that it is to be used.

His father instructed him to take the other four kings they caught that day to various people around town. "At that stage they used to give out the best cuts of deer and stuff to people, because Dad always said we could get more. Him and Grandma used to give out the food they put up in the summers, helped out a lot of people in town."

I commented on how different it is now by comparison with the way it was in Hoonah when he grew up.

"Everybody knew everybody down the line." He smiled. "We knew all the old-timers by name."

During the course of our conversation, a recent accident involving a couple of the local boys and a BB gun was brought up. I mentioned that I was wisely never allowed to own one growing up. Apparently his parents felt the same way about weapons and tools of mass destruction.

"My mom and dad always told us, no, you guys can't have that. We'd always make bows and arrows, and Dad would burn them up on us. We had darts one time, and Tom (his brother) got stuck, so Dad wouldn't allow darts in the house anymore."

I was once struck in the cheek by a dart by some neighbor kids across the alley; after that there seemed to be an ongoing struggle between us. I related how we used to hide in big cardboard boxes that we'd salvaged from the

Mike Mills

plumbing contractors down the street. The jerks across the alley would rain down pears on us, and when the thumping stopped, we'd rush out and start pitching them back up the hill.

Mike laughed. "With us, it was snowballs," he said. "When Skaflestad plowed the streets it would leave a high snow berm, so when the Salvation Army would come up the street and beat the drum, they'd be beating it, *Boom! Boom!* And all of a sudden, when they got by the house, *BOOM, BOOM, BOOM, BOOM, BOOM,* everybody was hitting the drum with snowballs."

When I could finally catch my breath, I asked if anyone got after them.

"Old man Joseph Pratt got pretty mad, and Robert Hanson Jr. was the drummer, but he couldn't catch us. We got disciplined by the uncles pretty much so we wouldn't have no hard feelings against our parents."

It would seem that a lot of hard feelings would be directed toward the uncles, but I guess that was what was preferred.

"I never got disciplined that much. I got in trouble a few times with Dad. We put a raft together without nails, and we were floating out here." He pointed to the beach.

"Well, how did it hold together?" I asked. "Did you just have ropes or what?"

"Didn't have nothing, just piled boards on boards. So Dad got a hold of us and dragged us all the way up the beach, all the way to the house by our ears, telling us, 'If you're not going to use them to listen, I'll make handles out of them.'" He laughed. "The next time I got in trouble with him was at Excursion. I was taking his bullets and throwing them in the furnace at the Philippino bunkhouse. Just sat there and watched them, *boom, boom, boom* — didn't even think about it. The furnace was on the outside of the building; it had a door, so I just opened the gate, threw a whole box in and run away."

"Did anyone get hurt?"

"No. Just me," he replied. "Got home, got spanked good." He chuckled.

It's stories like these that remind me that it's only God's grace that boys ever grow up to be men.

I hadn't realized that there was a separate bunkhouse for the Philippino workforce. Mike mentioned that the native workers were housed in a different area which was fenced in. According to him they weren't supposed to leave the compound while at Excursion, except to go to work. It sounded like segregation was still being practiced to some degree even after the Alaskan Anti-Discrimination Act was passed in the state in 1945. Prior to that, there were places throughout the state with signs declaring "no natives allowed" posted in public spaces. Understandably there was a feeling of distrust between the native and white populations, which I first experienced when I moved here, though at the time I had no idea why.

There were many interracial marriages, which in itself caused problems. For a number of years those who were of mixed descent didn't want to acknowledge their native roots. Mike and his brothers used to sneak up behind the house of one family and roll rocks down the hill against their house.

"They didn't like us; we didn't like them, either," he said.

"Why?"

"I don't know — we were natives, they weren't at the time. They didn't want to have any claim to be natives. We were called Siwashes and stuff."

"Siwash? What does that mean?"

"Like, dirty Indian or something."

I commented on how difficult it can be to live in a small town and not be able to get along with your neighbors, but I also understood the reality of the situation. I lived in an even smaller community where everyone was supposed to be like-minded, and we still had problems in abundance. It's just human nature, I guess.

Anyone who makes his or her living out on the water has to confront the possibility of running into foul weather. It's what makes commercial fishing one of the most dangerous occupations in the world. Everything is relative, I suppose, when it comes to weather and boats. Obviously a 100-foot crabber can easily take an ocean that would swamp a smaller vessel, like a troller, and a 32-foot troller would normally not be worried by waves that could sink an 18-foot skiff. I've often been surprised when battling my way back to port through white-capped waves to be confronted by a fellow in a skiff going out to where I've just come from, pounding the surf with his entire boat launched out of the water and crashing back down. I'm

The Greybeards

never sure if it's bravado or foolishness to be engaged in such an activity. On the day that Mike and I were talking, we had been experiencing a series of winter lows that left the water in turmoil. Mike mentioned that his main engine was broke down, but as soon as the weather broke, he was planning on going fishing with just his little engine, or kicker, as they are known. He mentioned possibly going across Icy Strait with just the small motor. With the weather so unstable, I asked if he wasn't afraid to go out.

"I was always told, don't let it scare you. Once it does, you got to stay home."

"There has to be weather that you don't go out in, though," I stated.

"Oh, yeah, common sense; if you get caught out in it, though, don't let it scare you. Dad said if you get in trouble to head for the beach. Find a spot and run up on the beach."

He recounted a time that he was fishing in Flynn Cove with his two young sons, Billy and Michael. He pulled out of the cove intent on running the few miles to Hoonah. There was a strong southeast wind blowing, and the waves were huge.

The boat was only a short distance from the boulder-strewn beach when his main engine quit. In danger of being driven up onto the rocks, he rushed to the stern where his small outboard was being washed over with the green water. He pulled the starter cord and ran hard back into Flynn Cove without waiting for the engine to warm up. They anchored up and spent the night in the skiff.

Mike Mills

When he went to start the engine the next morning, it wouldn't turn over.

Fortunately, his story ended well. For some, the outcome wasn't so favorable. According to Mike, Robert Hanson Jr., the Salvation Army drummer, drowned at Homeshore, along with his brother-in-law, when the power skiff they were in flipped over. There are two crosses on the bluffs marking the event. There are others as well who have paid the ultimate sacrifice. Three different men in three different skiffs come to mind, just in the time I've lived here. The sea is a harsh mistress; she can lure you with the promise of an abundant harvest, then once you've succumbed to her temptations, she'll change moods and punish you for daring to venture out. Yet, venture out we do; we really have no choice. If you're born a fisherman, whether growing up by the sea or an import from the Midwest, like myself, you have to answer the call of the ocean. It can be a difficult life, but for those who have chosen it, it's hard to imagine doing anything else.

Epilogue

Several years have passed since I first started working on this book — three, four, I really can't remember. With the passing of time things change. I'm afraid 2011 wasn't very kind to the friends and family of two of the men I've mentioned here. Karl Greenewald, the man who was sucked into the turbulent waters of North Inian Pass and survived, departed this life. He had been suffering with ill health and finally succumbed on January 1. With his passing another bit of Hoonah history is gone. I'm glad I was able to interview him and capture some of his memories before he left us.

On March 31 my friend Bunny, the good-natured man who loved fishing so much, left us after a battle with cancer. At the age of 59, his passing was much too soon. I do wish we could have talked one last time. I'm sure he had many a good story, and his company was always pleasant.

In January of 2012, we lost Windy Skaflestad. He'd been battling cancer for a few years. I was hoping he would get the better of it and join us once again on the fishing grounds, but it wasn't to be. Like the other two fishermen, he'll be sorely missed.

There are a few other transformations that should be mentioned here. Jim Dybdahl fished the *Coronation* for the last time this year. As per an agreement, he finished

Epilogue

out the season before turning her over to a new owner. The reliable old double-ender that served him so well the night of that awful storm on the Fairweather Grounds will have a new homeport and be guided by the hands of another captain. He is presently hoping to secure a freezer boat.

That rascal, the Hobbit, is still around, but his beloved boat, the *Judy Ann*, is not. Wooden boats need lots of TLC. A harsher environment than Southeast Alaska would be hard to find for a wooden boat. The constant freezing and thawing in the winter and the endless supply of freshwater that pounds the upper planks and decks eventually take a toll. The harbormaster determined it was no longer safe to have her in the harbor, and she was stripped and taken down the road to a rather unceremonious drop site where she was vandalized and picked apart like an animal carcass by vultures. It would have been more dignified if she had been burned. It wasn't a fitting end for a fine old boat. The Hobbit, by contrast, has fared much better. He's living in an apartment with three cats at the senior center. He doesn't get out much anymore. He traded his old van for a cat he took a liking to and now counts on the taxi to take him to the store or the occasional trip to the bar.

My neighbor Jake White spends most of his days inside. On occasion I see him and his wife, Lilly, hop in the car for a trip to the store or post office. With the beginning of a new year he'll soon be spending time on a hard bench at the high school gym watching our home

The Greybeards

team, the Braves, compete in a game of basketball. I've heard rumors that the *Mermaid* may be coming up for sale, but as of now it's just scuttlebutt.

Floyd Peterson is still operating a profitable business taking tourists out whale watching in the summer. When the tides are right and the weather permits, he fishes for king salmon during the winter. I'm never up early enough to see him leave, but I frequently see him come home, and I don't doubt that more often than not he's been successful.

I spot Adam Greenwald most often at the store or post office, sitting in his car with the heater on, listening to the Juneau radio station, waiting for his wife. If I tap on the glass, he'll roll down the window and we'll have a chat, and without fail he'll entertain me with some story from the past. I can always count on him to answer any question that I may have about fishing or Hoonah or the way things used to be.

Most days I pass Jerry and Caroline Peterson as they drive by in their truck. Brutus, their dog, is usually on the front seat or in Caroline's arms, no doubt happy that he doesn't have to withdraw to the punt in order to relieve himself. I'm not sure what their plans are concerning the upcoming fishing season, but I suspect the urge to do battle with some king salmon will arise as the spring approaches, and they will join me on the water.

As he's been doing for years, Mike Mills is still fishing from his skiff. I encounter him on occasion walking past the house, usually as he's going to or from his boat. I

Epilogue

believe his main motor has bit the dust, and he is waiting on a new one. Meanwhile, when the tides are right and the weather permits, he heads out with just his small trolling motor.

As for myself, my boat, the *Bonnie J*, is presently hauled out of the water and is undergoing a much needed replacement of the bow stem and multiple planks. She was built in 1945 and since I've had it, has seen quite a number of upgrades. Like old wooden boats, the shipwrights who work on them are becoming a thing of the past. Hoonah has been blessed to have an exceptional shipwright, John Kveum, living in her midst for a few years. I've been fortunate enough to have him work on the numerous and diverse projects that are giving the ol' *Bonnie J* a new lease on life.

Unlike my boat, I can't go in for an upgrade and be good as new. I have a bone disease that makes standing on my feet for too long a bit of a challenge, and I get tired easier now and can't put in the hours that the marathon seasons demand. I start and end each day with something hurting, but I can't imagine doing anything different. Will I someday echo the Hobbit and declare I've caught enough fish, or will I be like old Skippy Rude and stubbornly wrestle another season to the end? I don't know; time will tell. I just know that for now the memories of harvesting the sea makes my heart skip a beat, and God willing, I'll join my fellow fishermen, greybeards and newcomers alike in our annual pursuit.

References

Orth, Donald J., (1967) *Alaska Place Names; Geological Survey Professional Paper 567*, Washington, D.C.: United States Government Printing Office

Hembree, James and Students, (1973) *Hoonah History*, Alaska History Class 1973, Hoonah City Schools

Mackovjak, James, (2010) *Navigating in Troubled Waters — A History of Commercial Fishing in Glacier Bay, Alaska*, Gustavus, Alaska: US Department of the Interior, National Park Service, Glacier Bay National Park and Preserve

Cerveny, Lee K., (2007) *Sociocultural Effects of Tourism in Hoonah, Alaska*, General Technical Report PNW-GTR-734, Portland, Oregon; US Department of Agriculture, Forest Service, Pacific Northwest Research Station

Shcroeder, Robert F. and Kookesh, Matthew, (1990) *Subsistence Harvest and Use of Fish and Wildlife Resources and the Effects of Forest Management in Hoonah, Alaska, Technical Paper 142*, Juneau, Alaska: Division of Subsistence, Alaska Department of Fish and Game

References

Schroeder, Robert F. and Kookesh, Matthew, (1990) *Subsistence Harvest of Herring Eggs in Sitka Sound 1989, Technical Report 173*, Juneau, Alaska: Division of Subsistence, Alaska Department of Fish and Game

Carson, Norm, (2009) A Glimpse of Pelican's Beginning, Pelican, Alaska, Closest to the fish! Pelican.net

CHALCANTHITE (Hydrated Copper Sulphate)
www.Galleries.com/chalcanthite

Good Book Publishing
www.goodbookpublishing.com